Intergovernmental Relations in the 1980s

ANNALS OF PUBLIC ADMINISTRATION

Editor-in-Chief

JACK RABIN

Rider College
Lawrenceville, New Jersey

MARGARET ROSE, Assistant to the Editor-in-Chief

Managing Editors

GERALD J. MILLER   W. BARTLEY HILDRETH

University of Kansas   Kent State University
Lawrence, Kansas   Kent, Ohio

Topic Areas

A complete listing of editors' affiliations and editorial boards can be found at the end of this volume.

ANNALS OF PUBLIC ADMINISTRATION

Other Volumes in Preparation

Intergovernmental Relations in the 1980s

Edited by *RICHARD H. LEACH*

Duke University
Durham, North Carolina

MARCEL DEKKER, INC.   New York and Basel

Library of Congress Cataloging in Publication Data
Main entry under title:

Intergovernmental relations in the 1980s.

(Annals of public administration; 4)
Includes index.
1. Federal government—United States—Addresses,
essays, lectures. I. Leach, Richard H. II. Series.
JK325.I58   1983   321.02'0973   82-18321
ISBN 0-8247-1742-2

MARCEL DEKKER, INC.
270 Madison Avenue, New York, New York 10016

Current printing (last digit):
10 9 8 7 6 5 4 3 2 1

PRINTED IN THE UNITED STATES OF AMERICA

About the Series

The Annals of Public Administration is designed to present issues of topical concern to the public administration community. The series brings together the efforts of several hundred scholars and practitioners in twelve topic areas of public administration.

The goal of the Annals, therefore, is to encourage the most widespread dissemination of ideas. All volumes will be the product of the interaction between a topic-area editor for each topic area and a group of experts serving as both editorial board and advisors.

The topic areas to be covered in the Annals are:

1. Criminal Justice Administration
2. Health and Human Resources Administration
3. Implementation
4. Intergovernmental Relations
5. Organization Management
6. Policy Formulation and Evaluation
7. Public Administration Education
8. Public Administration History and Theory
9. Public Budgeting and Financial Management
10. Public Personnel Administration and Labor Relations
11. Regulation and Administrative Law
12. Research Methods in Public Administration

Because the series tries to remain up to date on current issues and topics in the field, it is quite important for the editor-in-chief and the topic-area editors to receive feedback from readers. What is your evaluation of the ways in which authors have approached the issues covered in a particular volume? What topics do you foresee will become important issues for the profession in the future? Please address your remarks to the topic-area editor and/or editor-in-chief.

We hope that the *Annals of Public Administration* will fulfill its goal and become a useful tool for the public administration community.

Jack Rabin

Preface

For a good many years now—at least ever since W. Brooke Graves edited an edition of the *Annals of the American Academy of Political and Social Science* intergovernmental relations have been recognized to be at the heart of American federalism and the way programs are administered and implemented therein. Under the Reagan administration especially, the relations among the various levels and units of American government are being examined and questioned. Indeed, President Reagan has promised to redefine federalism in the United States and some of that redefinition is already influencing policy. It may well be that the intergovernmental pattern we have come to know—and some to deplore—over the last two or more decades is about to be fundamentally altered.

The chapters in this volume of the *Annals* were commissioned of leading scholars in the field of federalism and intergovernmental relations. They were asked to direct their thinking to the present status and future course of these relations so as to provide some guidance as to what to expect as Reagan federalism unfolds. There is a diversity of opinion among the authors which suits the subject admirably inasmuch as diversity is among the enduring and endearing characteristics of American federalism. In any case, adaptions can be expected in the future as they have been made in the past, for federalism is a flexible form of government, capable of adjusting to changes in the nation itself. Perhaps the chapters in this volume will provide some understanding of the next series of changes likely to be made in the intergovernmental pattern under which we conduct our governmental business. The volume would have been enriched by an article on intergovernmentalism and education by Joel S. Berke of the Education Policy Research Institute. Unfortunately, Dr. Berke died suddenly before the article could be completed. This volume is dedicated to his memory.

Richard H. Leach

Contributors

George S. Blair Department of Government, Claremont Graduate School, Claremont, California

Robert F. Carmody Procurement, Acquisition, and Grants Management Program, The American University, Washington, D.C.

Jerome J. Hanus School of Government and Public Administration, The American University, Washington, D.C.

Catherine H. Lovell Graduate School of Administration, University of California, Riverside, California

David B. Walker Government Structure and Function Section, U.S. Advisory Commission of Intergovernmental Relations, Washington, D.C.

John W. Winkle III Department of Political Science, University of Mississippi, University, Mississippi

Deil S. Wright Department of Political Science, University of North Carolina at Chapel Hill, Chapel Hill, North Carolina

Contents

Intergovernmental Relations in the 1980s

1

A Perspective on Intergovernmental Relations

David B. Walker   U.S. Advisory Commission on Intergovernmental Relations, Washington, D.C.

With the advent of the new "New Federalism" of President Ronald Reagan, American federalism turned a definite corner and began on a very different course from that which it had pursued for the previous 2, if not 5, decades. Its goals of ending deficits, developing a dynamic economy, devolving powers and programs to the states and localities, and attempting deregulation highlight this basic shift in direction.

NO HARKENING BACK TO HOOVER

Yet, Reagan federalism with its heavily devolutionary and deregulating thrusts, even if fully implemented, involves no real return to the dual federalist principles and practices of the Hoover era. The economic, social, judicial, and political developments that produced an ever-mounting tendency to focus on Washington during the past 50 and especially the last 20 years preclude any return to the fairly distinct separation of governmental functions, powers, and finance by governmental level that prevailed in the late 1920s.* Moreover, the Reagan

*In the opinion of this writer, the 15 federal grant programs representing 2% of all state revenues in 1927 and even the growing federal regulatory role constituted no significant undermining of Madison's essentially compartmentalized system, since nearly all of the growing number of public services were enacted, performed, and funded exclusively by state and local governments, and since few of the states' police, interstate commerce, or taxing powers were denied or even seriously countered by the national government's regulatory actions.

1

"safety net" principle, along with the administration's support of various subsidy programs, symbolizes its acceptance of much of the New Deal.

NO RETURN TO EISENHOWER

In addition, there seems little likelihood of any real return to the simpler and fairly stabilized intergovernmental relations of 1960. One hundred and thirty-two grant programs involving only $7.02 billion, focusing chiefly on four functional areas (highways, old age assistance, aid to dependent children, and employment security)* and involving almost wholly a federal-state relationship,[†] constituted no major federal instrusion in intergovernmental relations. Moreover, the fact that these grants did *not* affect much more than half of the states' services (and only two significantly), any traditional municipal services, and the vast majority of the counties' or any of the school districts' activities[‡] further underscores the modest level of this interpenetration. Therefore, any serious effort to restore it would flounder on the rocks of contemporary political and fiscal reality.

The same can be said regarding the drive for deregulation. The expansion of the federal government's regulatory role during the period from 1933 to 1960 (for the first time in agriculture, stock exchanges, public utility holding companies, and atomic energy, and in an extended way in communication, shopping, and airlines) and of its historic function as broker-subsidizer of key interest groups[§] was aimed fairly clearly at interstate issues involving the private sector. Thus, unlike today's situation, it had no significant intergovernmental regulatory component, and it did not in any way severely circumscribe the states' police powers. All this clearly is in marked contrast to the massive assignment covering both the private and the state and local sectors that the Reagan administration's deregulation effort has taken on.

In short, the federal system of 1960 was only moderately intergovernmentalized, fairly inexpensive, and relatively uncomplicated, despite some criticisms of program duplication, grant conditions (especially of the single-state agency requirements), and allocational formulas. Cooperative federalism, then, with its "marble-cake" metaphor, was an apt description of the system. A marble cake, after all, involves only two kinds of batter, and its weavings,

---

*These four accounted for almost three-quarters of the federal aid total in 1960.
[†] All but 8% of federal aid in 1960 went to the states.
[‡] The impacted area programs were essentially "no strings" grants.
[§] One hundred forty such subsidy programs were operational in 1960, almost 90% of which had been enacted between 1930 and 1960.

though convoluted and swirling, are nevertheless comparatively few and clearly discernible* [1].

Overall, then, it was a balanced, buoyant, and functioning system, about which the bulk of the electorate was sanguine. And this, despite serious malapportionment in most of its legislative systems and despite its obvious failure to combat successfully racial segregation.

While the positive attributes of the system of 2 decades ago obviously are attractive to the administration and to many others, the Reagan efforts thus far suggest no literal attempt to return to the comparatively placid and politically consensual period of Eisenhower. Additionally, the emerging Reagan record on civil rights does not suggest a desire to retreat to the years before the enactment of the Civil and Voting Rights Acts of the 1960s; and the administration's retrenchment, curbing of regulations, capping of entitlement programs, and consolidation efforts do not combine to produce the relatively low level of federal intervention in the federal system that prevailed 2 decades ago.

HOW NEW?

In what sense, then, is the new "New Federalism" new? It is new in the sense that it (1) takes issue with most of the mushrooming intergovernmental developments that began in the mid-1960s and escalated throughout the 1970s; (2) postulates an almost wholly devolutionary approach (unlike Nixonian New Federalism) to achieving its prescribed cure of intergovernmental decongestion; and (3) already has indicated a clear capacity to achieve some of its specific reform proposals.

The recent developments against which Reagan federalism is directed include the following:

1. *The rapidly accelerating flow of federal aid dollars,* including a doubling of the amount under Johnson's Creative Federalism, another doubling under Nixon's New Federalism, a 41% hike during President Ford's brief tenure, and a 53% rise with President Carter's New Partnership Federalism. All told, more than a 12-fold increase occurred in federal grant outlays between 1960 and 1980 (from $7.1 to $91.5 billion); even in constant dollar terms, there still was a doubling of the funds between 1968 and 1980.

2. *A proliferation in the number of programs,* with 209 new grants enacted during the Great Society period, another 90-odd during the Nixon-Ford

*It was, however, a less appropriate one for state-local relationships, given the far greater level of interpenetration and interdependency that had emerged in this sector since the 1930s. State aid to localities increased by a factor of 10 between 1932 and 1958; 124 new state revenue enactments took place; and the number of state mandates began to rise.

era, and approximately 70 more during the Carter years—for a total by the end of 1980 of over 530 authorized and funded grants, and this despite consolidations involving some 46 categorical grants.

3. *A massive expansion in program initiatives,* which encompassed an array of wholly new federal endeavors (e.g., regional economic development, medical assistance for the poor, antipoverty measures, primary and secondary education, and energy conservation) and of major expansions of older programs (e.g., Aid to Families with Dependent Children, natural resources and the environment, transportation, programs for the aged, and public health). This aid package by 1980 continued to include grants in functional areas deemed by many to be wholly national concerns (i.e., a costly cluster of income maintenance and a smaller group of employment security programs) as well as a lengthy list of grants for purposes deemed in 1960 to be wholly state or local concerns (e.g., fire protection, libraries, police pensions, bikeways, noise control, and solid waste disposal). In addition to the above reasons for the ever-mounting number of programs, the congressional (and interest group) tendency, especially during the 1970s, to subfunctionalize aided program areas and to hyperspecify even within these narrowly defined areas must be reckoned with. (These programs included 20 social services, 22 health services, 50 primary and secondary education, 13 food and nutrition, and 11 highway safety programs).

4. *An explosion in the kinds and number of eligible grant recipients,* thanks to (a) the growth in direct federal-local grants under Creative Federalism (accounting for 12% of total grant funds by 1968); (b) their somewhat ironic increase under New Federalism, due to General Revenue Sharing (GRS) and two federal-local block grants—the Comprehensive Employment and Training Act of 1973 (CETA) and the Community Development Block Grants (CDBG) of 1974, which brought the "bypassing" proportion to 24% by 1974; which brought the "bypassing" proportion to 24% by 1974; and (c) to the steady congressional tendency during the 1970s of responding to all manner of local representational efforts, both public and private. Thus by 1977 (the last year for all three of the congressionally initiated, locally focused countercyclical programs) 28% of federal aid went directly to local units of government or nonprofit bodies.* By 1980, the predominant federal-state partnership pattern of 2 decades earlier had become one wherein all states, all counties, all cities and towns, nearly all school districts, and at least half of the special districts, along with about 1800 substate regional units, hundreds of nonprofit units, and dozens of colleges and universities were direct recipients of federal aid funds, and this in addition to the *one-fifth* of state aid in any recent year

---

* This receded to about a quarter of the total by 1980.

which represented federal aid channeled through the states and then to localities (chiefly to counties and school districts) [2,3].

5. *The apparent but not authentic emergence of a tripartite aid system,* under which, in addition to the categorical grants, five block grants were enacted between 1966 and 1974 (Partnership for Health, 1966; the Safe Streets Act, 1968; Social Services, 1972; CETA, 1973; and CDBG, 1974) and the first general support grant (GRS) came into being in 1972. Yet the heavy outlays for categorical grants never were really threatened—the low point being 75% of the 1975 aid total with a rise to about 80% by 1980. Moreover, both the block grants and GRS over time acquired conditions, requirements, and/or earmarks rendering them something less than "few strings" and "no strings" programs, though they still were less constrained in terms of recipient discretion than most categorical grants.

6. The *advent of a new era of federal intergovernmental regulation* [4] reflected in (a) the enactment or promulgation of some 60 national policy objectives applicable to all or most grant programs (nondiscrimination, environmental protection, health and safety, labor and procurement standards, and so forth, (b) the partial preemption by the federal government of certain state and local activities wherein the national government established basic policies or standards but assigned administrative responsibility to the states or localities (e.g., the Water Quality Act of 1965 and the Clean Air Act Amendments of 1970), (c) the growing use of "crossover sanctions" in specific grants under which the failure to comply with the requirements of one aid program could lead to a reduction or termination of funds from other, usually related programs (e.g., the Highway Beautification Act of 1965 and the Emergency Highway Energy Conservation Act of 1974), and (d) direct mandates which take the form of legal orders to states or local governments which must be complied with under threat of criminal or civil penalties (e.g., the Equal Employment Opportunity Act of 1972 and the Fair Labor Standards Act Amendments of 1974* [5].

7. The *establishment of hundreds of quasi-governmental substate regional units, almost 20 multistate bodies, and countless new agencies* within state and local governments, either directly or indirectly as a result of federal grant conditions. There the enactment of more than 20 federal grants programs (Safe Streets, economic development, health planning, coastal zone management, metropolitan transportation, air and water quality, and so on) that prompted the creation of 1600 to 1800 single-purpose, multicounty planning bodies and the advent of nine multistate economic development and eight river basin commissions should be noted. At the substate regional level, congressional and administrative requirements mandated a review and comment process in metro-

*This was overturned by the now famous case of *National League of Cities* v. *Usery.*

politan areas and encouraged it in nonmetropolitan areas, thus causing a dramatic, 33-fold increase in regional councils. Yet, at least half of these units have not been designated to carry out the functions of the other federal regional programs in their respective areas.

8. The *growing reliance by states and localities on federal aid funds*, hiking federal grants as a percentage of state-local expenditures from 14.7% in 1960 to 19.4% by 1970, to 26.4% in 1978, and finally down slightly to 26.3% by 1980. Note also the significant increases between 1957 and 1978 in direct federal aid as a percentage of local own source revenues: 1.2 to 19.2% for counties, 1.4 to 25.0% for cities, 2.3 to 3.7% for school districts, and 8.9 to 34.0% for special districts.

9. The *crucial emergence of Congress during the 1970s as the master architect and arbiter of an increasingly dysfunctional intergovernmental system,* thanks to its hyperresponsiveness to all manner of interest group pressures, the ingenuity of its many entrepreneurial members, its use of categorical grants and conditions to pacify highly divergent groups, and its tendency to convert the reauthorization process (for Great Society programs especially) into an omnibus vehicle for expansionist programmatic and regulatory goals [6, 7] .

10. Finally, the *ever-expanding role of the federal judiciary* as a not-so-judicious umpire of the system, with the basic trend in the courts' grant-related decisions being toward a reaffirmation of Congress' power to spend in the advancement of the general welfare, rarely checking Congress' power to attach almost any variety of condition to grants, and invariably toward leaving the protection of the Tenth Amendment almost wholly to national political processes and to the capacity of recipient governments to refuse participation in grants. At the same time, the National League of Cities and lower court EPA (Environmental Protection Agency) cases suggest that a latitudinarian congressional exercise of the commerce power can lead to the gradual erosion of the states as quasi-sovereign political entities. Some sense of intergovernmental "comity" was reflected in certain Supreme Court decisions during the 1970s relating to state judicial proceedings.

These 10 trends combined by 1980 to produce a transformed intergovernmental system—one that was overloaded with congestion at the center and at the peripheries and along the countless avenues of contact [7, 8] . By 1980, it was a system wherein federal policies had spilled over into nearly every program area, almost every regulatory field, and almost seven-eights of the 80,000 subnational governments. But it also was a system wherein the direct servicing role of the national government was nearly the same as it was 40 years earlier*; thus the size of the federal bureaucracy tended to remain relatively static and

*Medicare and the supplementary security income program were the only major exceptions to this generalization.

small. In short, expansionism in federal policies and in program entitlements and continuing federal constraint regarding its bureaucracy and direct imple- mentation efforts combined to constitute the two basic reasons for the in- creasingly dysfunctional condition of American federalism in the 1970s. The liberalism implicit in the former clearly is a Reagan administration concern, but the continuing conservatism reflected in the latter is much less so.

THE STATE ROLE: CHANGES AND CHALLENGES (1966 to 1980)

Were the states undermined or eclipsed by this decade and a half of incessant federal intergovernmental interventionism? The answer essentially is "no," though with a few qualifiers. And the basically positive nature of this response figures prominently in the devolutionary design of Reagan federalism, since the states are the preferred partners in its scenario.

Three factors during the past 2 decades—indigenous reform efforts, fed- erally triggered legislative reapportionment along with voting rights changes, and the emerging role of the states in the system as the prime intermediate level managers and partial funders of the largest intergovernmental aid programs— combined in the 1970s to thrust them into the mainstream of intergovern- mental developments and of the system's overall operations. This general trend, however, was not clearly understood in Washington or sometimes among the nation's localities, although it obviously was and is not overlooked by the Rea- gan federalists.

One of the most prominent manifestations of the changed condition of the states was the major overhaul of their governmental structures and process- es. Between 1960 and 1980, five constitutions were completely overhauled, and several others were subjected to major amendment; 11 states gave their governors 4-year terms (for a total of 46); six adopted a "short ballot" for state executive officers (bringing the total to nine); 23 major executive board reorganizations were instituted (1965 to 1979); the proportion of state employees covered by some form of merit system rose from 50 to 75%; the number of legislatures operating on a biennial basis was reduced from 31 to 14 (with the 14 usually meeting in special session in the second year); and the number of state judi- ciaries having most of the basic traits of a reformed and integrated system soar- ed from 3 in 1960 to about 37. In short, the reshaping of the structures of state government moved at a fast pace during these 2 decades—reflecting the new and expanded political, functional, and intergovernmental roles they were assuming.

Parallel to this was the transformation of state revenue systems, with the adoption of a personal income tax by 11, a corporate income levy by 9, and a general sales tax by 9. These 29 enactments produced a state revenue picture in 1981 in which 40 had a broad—based income tax; 45, a corporate income tax; and a comparable number, a general sales tax—with 36 generally using all three, compared to 19 only 20 years earlier. Although many cuts and few increases in rates have been enacted since 1976 and although lids on expenditures or revenues have been instituted in 18 states, overall, their revenue systems clearly are more diversidied and resilient than their predecessors of the earlier period.

Yet another prime sign of the states' strengthened position is the role they have assumed, partly as a result of national grant-in-aid actions and partially as a result of their own actions, as pivotal intermediate level planners, supervisors, partial funders, and sometimes direct providers of large, expensive, and significant intergovernmental programs. As the recipients in any recent fiscal year of 75 to 80% of all federal aid, as the subnational jurisdictional group that is most involved with major federal grants having heavy matching or cost-sharing requirements (e.g., Medicaid and AFDC), and as the senior financier of certain local services (notably primary and secondary education), the states almost unknowingly have assumed a new and well understood (either (by Washington or their localities) function in the overall federal system of planning, controlling, and partially or heavily funding big intergovernmental programs [9, 10]. This role obviously would be expanded under Reagan federalism.

How have the strengthening of the structures of state government, of their revenue basis, and of their operational role in the system affected directly or indirectly their localities? Based on the record of the 50 states, the following general findings emerge:

State aid soared (experiencing almost a ninefold increase between 1960 and 1980), but the bulk of it was focused on the four traditionally assisted areas (education, welfare, highways, and health/hospitals), and this meant that school districts and counties were its chief local recipients.

Federal "pass-through the states" aid to localities rose from $7.3 billion (estimated in 1971 to 1972 to $12.3 billion in 1976 to 1977; the functional breakdown, however, of most of this financial assistance (education, $5.2 billion; public welfare, $5.0 billion; health/hospitals, $413 million; highways, $232 million; and all other, $1.5 billion) in 1977 again indicates that school districts and counties (and to a lesser degree, special districts) were the chief substate beneficiaries, not cities, providing regular municipal services.

Property tax relief was instituted (28 of the states financed a "circuit breaker" variety) in recognition of the fact that income, sales, and property are but three angles of one state-local financial triangle (and the local property tax angle had been too large).

There was a greater propensity for states to assume directly the performance of certain new responsibilities as well as to mandate a shift upward of certain local functions.

Greater discretion was given cities and counties to adopt alternatives forms of government, to enter into interlocal service agreements, and, to a much lesser degree, to transfer functions.

A growing tendency emerged to mandate local servicing levels, the conditions of local public employment, and sometimes new functions—more often than not without the "fiscal note" warning device.

Only modest expansions were made in allowing cities and counties all functional powers not denied by state constitutions or statutes, in permitting greater local revenue diversification, in liberalizing annexation statutes, and in curbing special district formation.

These recent state-local trends combine to suggest that the states during the period from 1960 to 1980 continued to pursue the course of increasing interdependency that was carved out in the postwar years. But with greater reason than the federal government! The states, after all, were and are the legal source of the structure, powers, and finances as well as the overall jurisdictional pattern of the nation's localities, in that the state-local relationship is one that operates within the context of a unitary system. Moreover, while some of the above findings can be viewed negatively from a local perspective, it also seems clear generally that the earlier state role of the "neglectful parent" has been pretty much scrapped. Finally, while from both the state and local perspectives a much more intricate pattern of interdependency has emerged, this is reflected in 50 quite different state and local fiscal and servicing systems [11]. This rather obvious operational fact of American federalism was frequently overlooked in the drafting of federal grant legislation and regulations, but it would appear to be a crucial conditioner of Reagan federalism goals.

REAGAN FEDERALISM (1981-   )

The election in 1980 of Ronald Reagan as president and of a Republican Senate and the emergence of a conservative coalition in the nominally Democratic House heralded the emergence of a counterforce ready to do battle with the political and especially the pressure group dynamics that during the 1970s focused chiefly on the Congress and produced the dysfunctional federal interventionism described earlier. In effect, the new administration accepted the diagnosis of the Advisory Commission on Intergovernmental Relations, the National Governors Association, the National Conference of State Legislatures, and others that the system was seriously overloaded. But unlike these groups which found congestion at the center and at the peripheries [7], Reagan federalism discovered it chiefly at the center. Consequently, and in contrast with Nixonian New Federalism, it has focused almost wholly on devolutionary programs and goals with the exception of the proposed federalization of Medicaid.

Thus far, the three prime and interrelated prescriptions of the Reagan New Federalism are (1) to develop a dynamic, but noninflation-plagued economy, (2) to devolve programs, power, and funding sources ultimately to the states and localities, and (3) to deregulate or at least to curb overregulation. The Reagan budget and tax packages obviously were geared primarily to the first goal. Yet part of the massive budget offensive were cuts in grants (usually at the 25% level for fiscal year 1982), no appropriations for at least 90 categorical programs, and seven proposed block grants adhering to the "special revenue sharing" format (i.g., very few conditions).* In short, a major secondary effect of the 1981 battle of the budget was to further the devolution goal, with the block grants being described by the administration as transitional—to be followed eventually by a turnback of revenue sources.

As of early June 1981, the fate of nearly all of the block grant proposals was in doubt, thanks to Senate modifications and major amendatory or wholly rejectionist House committee actions. With the advent of Gramm-Latta II and the House conservative coalition's drive to convert the budgetary reconciliation process into a vehicle for achieving program changes, the block grant initiatives took on new life. The president's social services and community development proposals reemerged in roughly recognizable form, although political maneuvering required the adoption of a much more limited approach to the health services and preventive health block grants.

From the massive conference committee, nine block grants emerged: community development (a block grant to the states for nonentitlement local jurisdictions covered previously by the discretionary grant portion of the earlier CDBG program, with the 701 planning grant being folded into both); elementary and secondary education (combining 37 categorical grants); Preventive Health and Health Services (6 categorical grants and the old Partnership for Health block grant); Alcohol, Drug Abuse, and Mental Health (6 categoricals); Maternal and Child Health (9 categoricals); Primary Care (2 categorical); Social Services (1 categorical and the Title XX block grant); Community Services (7 categoricals); and Low Income Home Energy Assistance (1 categorical).

None of the nine was what the administration initially called for—either in coverage or in grant design. Seventy-one categorical grants and two earlier block grants were merged, but at least 50 that the presidents' initial proposals would have merged were excluded. All nine go to the states, but with a required 80% pass-through requirement in the new education grant, an earmark-

*The last involved the consolidation of some 115 aid programs into social services (20), health services (22), preventive health services (12), energy and emergency assistance (2), local special education needs (15), state programs for elementary and secondary education (35), and a new community development (9) block grant.

ing of certain funds for a pass-through in both the Primary Care and Community Services grants, and the stipulation in the Community Development grant that either certain conditions, including a 10% match, must be met by the participating states or the earlier federal-local relationship would continue.

The increased state role here is further underscored when it is recognized that 51 of the 73 merged grants went to local governments and nonprofits either exclusively or in addition to state agencies. Given the functional focus of these grants, counties, school districts, and nonprofits will be more affected by this shift in relationships than cities—save in those instances in which municipalities perform county-type functions or possess dependent school districts.

All nine meet critical criteria of a block grant—with greater discretion given to recipients than was the case with the predecessor categorical grants. There are variations among the nine, however, and none incorporates all the "special revenue sharing" features of the president's initial proposals. Witness the following:

States under all nine must make available to the public a plan on how funds will be used.

Under eight, a public hearing is called for.

Eight (Primary Care excepted) require no federal agency prior approval of state applications or statements of intended use.

Three (Maternal and Child Health, Primary Care, and CDBG) require a nonfederal match, and another three include a "maintenance of effort" provision (Education; Preventive Health and Health Services; and Alcohol, Drug Abuse, and Mental Health). leaving three with neither (Social Services, Community Services, and Low-Income Home Energy Assistance).

Regarding reporting, one (Social Services) requires biennially a report of fund use; four require an annual report, but the secretary in each is directed to avoid making this condition "burdensome"; two stipulate a report to the public rather than the disbursing federal agency; while two (Community Development and Education) give the relevant secretaries power to specify reporting requirements.

Curbing grant outlays, in effect, is another facet of Reagan federalism's devolutionary drive. The cuts in various of the aid programs—including nearly all of the blocks*—constitute more than a continuation of the tapering-off trend reflected in the last two Carter budgets. Actual reductions are involved, after all, with a real rollback from the estimated $95 billion total in FY 1980 to about $87 billion in FY 1982. Linked to the cuts were authorization actions calling for no appropriations for fiscal years 1982 to 1984 for at least 60 categorical programs.

*The older CDBG program and the local share of GRS were not cut.

Turning to the deregulation goal, the new administration soon established a cabinet-level task force on regulatory relief, chaired by Vice President Bush. Some 34 of 104 actions taken during the spring of 1981 provided relief to state and local governments, and some 18 additional actions were taken after the feverish first hundred days. Moreover, during the initial efforts to explain the newly enacted block grants, administration spokespersons made it clear that few if any requirements—other than those called for in the legislation—would be imposed administratively. Yet a full scale effort to reform federal regulations in their multiple manifestations must involve the Congress, the real source of most of the regulatory proliferation and, of course, the courts.

To conclude, it is too early to describe all of the features of Reagan federalism and their impact on the system. Some additional thrusts no doubt will emerge from the deliberations of the president's Federalism Advisory Committee. Moreover, the full effects of what already has been accomplished, as well as the outcome of promised new initiatives in the program cutback, grant consolidation, and revenue turnback areas, also are tough to forecast. Whether alternative approaches to decongesting the system will gain strength is also problematic. The Advisory Commission on Intergovernmental Relations, the National Governors' Association, the National Conference of State Legislatures, and some local organizations have urged a sorting out of some of the major program responsibilities by govermental level—with some, such as welfare and Medicaid, being federalized, and others, such as education and highways, being turned over to the states.

What is predictable is that the cuts in federal aid are real and will be felt; that the fiscal, political, and management pressures on the states will mount; that many local jurisdictions, particularly cities in the northeast and Great Lakes areas, will confront especially difficult challenges; that the success of many of the administration's New Federalism thrusts depends heavily on the success of its economic program; and that the state-local connection will become even stronger.

REFERENCES

1. Walker, David B. *Toward A Functioning Federalism*, Winthrop Publishers, Inc., Cambridge, Mass., (1981). pp. 76-77.
2. Advisory Commission on Intergovernmental Relations (ACIR) (1980). *Recent Trends in Federal and State Aid to Local Governments* (Report M-118), U.S. Government Printing Office, Washington, D.C. pp. 27-28.
3. Stephens, G. Ross, and Gerald W. Olson (August 1, 1979). *Pass-Through Federal Aid and Interlevel Finance in the American Federal System, 1957-77,* Volume 1, a report to the National Science Foundation, NSA/APR 77000348, University of Missouri-Kansas City, pp. 31-56.

4. Beam, David R. (Summer 1981). Washington's regulation of states and localities: origins and issues, *Intergovernmental Perspective*, Volume 7, Number 3, Advisory Commission on Intergovernmental Relations, Washington, D.C.
5. *National League of Cities* v. *Usery* (1976) 426 U.S. 833.
6. Walker, David B. (1981). *Toward A Functioning Federalism*, Winthrop Publishers, Inc., Cambridge, Mass., pp. 223-247.
7. Advisory Commission on Intergovernmental Relations (ACIR) (1981). *An Agenda for American Federalism: Restoring Confidence and Competence* (Report A-86), U.S. Government Printing Office, Washington, D.C. pp. 9-32).
8. Barfield, Claude E. (July 1, 1981). Rethinking Federalism, unpublished draft report to the American Enterprise Institute.
9. Walker, David B. (Fall 1980). The states and the system: changes and choices, *Intergovernmental Perspective*, Volume 6, Number 4, Advisory Commission on Intergovernmental Relations, Washington, D.C.
10. Beer, Samuel H. (Fall 1973). The modernization of american federalism, *Publius*, Volume 3, Number 2, Center for the Study of Federalism, Temple University, Philadelphia, Pa., pp. 81-87.
11. Advisory Commission on Intergovernmental Relations (ACIR) (1981). *State and Local Roles in the Federal System*, U.S. Government Printing Office, Washington, D.C. Chap. 2.

2

Intergovernmental Relations in the 1980s
A New Phase of IGR

Deil S. Wright University of North Carolina at Chapel Hill,
Chapel Hill, North Carolina

It is an accepted fact that since 1900 the U.S. political system has experienced significant changes that border on major but evolutionary upheavals. One approach to systematizing and understanding the events and shifts of nearly a century-long period of national-state-local relationships is to think of phases of IGR (intergovernmental relations). This approach has been elaborated elsewhere [1]. The aim here is to identify and explore only the most recent and current phase of IGR—the calculative phase. A short sketch of the five previous phases will provide a basis for exploring the current calculative phase.

The six phases of IGR and their approximate periods of prominence are:

Conflict:	pre-1930s
Cooperative:	1930s to 1950s
Concentrated:	1940s to 1960s
Creative:	1950s to 1960s
Competitive:	1960s to 1970s
Calculative:	1970s to 1980s

A condensed chart of the distinctive features of each phase is provided in Table 1.

For each phase of IGR three substantive components are identified. (See the second through fourth columns of Table 1.) First, what policy issues dominated the public agenda during each phase? Second, what dominant percep-

Table 1 Phases of Intergovernmental Relations (IGR)

Phase descriptor	Main problems	Participants perceptions	IGR mechanisms	Federalism metaphor	Approximate climax period
Conflict	Defining boundaries Proper spheres	Antagonistic Adversary Exclusivity	Statutes Courts Regulations	Layer-cake federalism	19th Century-1930s
Cooperative	Economic distress International threat	Collaboration Complimentarity Mutuality Supportive	National planning Formula grants Tax credits	Marble-cake federalism	1930s-1950s
Concentrated	Service needs Physical development	Professionalism Objectivity Neutrality Functionalism	Categorical grants Service standards	Water taps (focused or channeled)	1940s-1960s
Creative	Urban-metropolitan Disadvantaged clients	National goals Great Society Grantsmanship	Program planning Project grants Participation	Flowering (proliferated and fused)	1950s-1960s
Competitive	Coordination Program effectiveness Delivery systems Citizen access	Disagreement Tension Rivalry	Grant consolidation Revenue sharing Reorganization	Picket fence (fragmented)	1960s-1970s
Calculative	Accountability Bankruptcy Constraints Dependency Federal Role Public confidence	Gamesmanship Fungibility Overload	General aid-entitlements Bypassing Loans Crosscutting regulations	Facade (confrontational)	1970s-1980s

Source: Wright, 1982, p. 45.

tions did the chief participants seem to have? What orientations or mind-sets guided their behavior in each phase? Third, what mechanisms and techniques were used to implement intergovernmental actions and objectives during each period? The fifth column of the table lists a metaphorical characterization of each phase. The metaphors most commonly used are forms of federalism.

The dates for each period are approximate at best. Indeed, the phases actually overlap. Therefore, the idea of climax period is important—not only because it conveys a time of peak prominence but because it does not preclude the continuation of a phase beyond the dates given. For example, although the conflict phase climaxed before and during the 1930s, conflict patterns did not end then. They regularly recur today as subsidiary events during the current dominant calculative phase.

Thus, like successive, somewhat porous strata that have been superimposed on each other (by the interactions and perspectives of public officials), no phase ends at an exact point—nor does it in fact disappear. Each phase is continuously present in greater or lesser measure, bearing the weight, so to speak, of the overlying strata (subsequent phases) and producing carry-over effects much wider than the climax periods indicated in Table 1. Indeed, the present state of IGR results from multiple overlays of each of the six phases. The task of an IGR analyst is like that of a geologist: to drill or probe the several strata and from the samples make inferences about the substructure of the terrain.

Short sketches of the first five phases serve as backdrops for the more extended analysis of the sixth phase. The conflict, cooperative, concentrated, creative, and competitive phases are reviewed below.

CONFLICT PHASE

Until the 1930s the relationships between the national, state, and local governments were known largely for the conflicts they generated. Courts, legislative bodies, and elected executives seemed to be propelled by concerns over who had the "right" to act (or not act) on a problem, such as regulating child labor, promoting public health, or assuring a minimum standard of welfare. Various governmental bodies made an effort to define clearly the boundaries and "proper" spheres of action of local, state, and national governments. Scholars have correctly noted that submerged below the prominent conflicts were elements of cooperation [2, 3]. Nevertheless, it was common to use a culinary metaphor in describing IGR prior to and into the 1930s—layer-cake federalism.

COOPERATIVE PHASE

The economic distress of the 1930s and the international demands and tensions of the 1940s brought public officials together in a spirit of cooperation.

Collaboration between the national government and the states in the welfare field was a noteworthy result of the Depression. All governments and officials, of course, supported the war effort of 1941 to 1945. One perceptive observer [4] noted that:

> cooperative government by federal-state-local authorities has become a byword in the prodigious effort to administer civilian defense, rationing, and other war-time programs. Intergovernmental administration, while it is a part of all levels of government, is turning into something quite distinct from them all.

The degree of cooperation between national, state, and local officials in administrative affairs did not stop at the end of World War II. The continuing intertwining of IGR contacts gave rise to a new metaphor—marble-cake federalism.

CONCENTRATED PHASE

IGR became increasingly concentrated around a rising number of specific federal grant-in-aid programs. Over 20 major functional, highly focused grant programs were established in a 15-year postwar period, including programs for airports, defense education, libraries, sewage treatment, and urban renewal. The number, focus, fiscal size, and specificity of these grant programs produced an incremental but distinct policy shift in national-state and national-local relations.

The contacts now involved or were even dominated by exchanges between specialists and professionals in particular fields, such as airport engineering, library science, and health. Administrators, who were also program professionals, entered the scene as important participants. This rising professionalism was reflected in the entire public service and is the reason this phase is labeled *"concentrated."* Mosher has referred to the 1950s as the "triumph of the professional state" [5].

In addition, between 1953 and 1955 a temporary presidential commission devoted considerable attention to policy and administrative questions involving IGR. Continuing attention to IGR has been assured since 1959, when the Congress created the permanent Advisory Commission on Intergovernmental Relations (ACIR). The ACIR is a representative body that conducts studies and makes recommendations to improve the functioning of the federal system. It is composed of 26 members: 3 private citizens, 9 national officials (3 each from the executive branch, House, and Senate), and 14 representatives of state and local governments.

CREATIVE PHASE

The cooperative and concentrated phases constituted the pilings if not the full foundation on which the creative phase of IGR was erected. The word for this phase comes from President Johnson's Great Society era, when he called for numerous program and policy initiatives under the banner of "Creative Federalism." The impact of the Johnson initiatives on IGR was stupendous. Over a hundred major new categorical grant programs were enacted (nearly 300 specific legislative authorizations). More significant from an administrative point of view was that the bulk of the new grant authorizations were *project* grants. Historically, most grants had formula provisions that apportioned the grant monies among the states (or occasionally among cities). But project grant funds for programs such as Model Cities and Urban Mass Transit were available for open competition, so to speak. Large numbers of cities could (and did) apply with specific and detailed project proposals, which were required to fit guidelines and regulations. Not only did federal program administrators write the regulations, but they also made most (if not all) of the decisions on which cities' projects were approved and funded. State and local administrators were similarly thrust into the policy-making limelight, in part because of the additional resources available to them and the clientele-building tasks needed to sustain new programs.

The revolution in IGR during the 1960s can be noted in financial terms. Federal aid to state and local governments more than tripled from $7 billion in 1960 to about $24 billion in 1970. A similar increase also characterized state aid to local units—from almost $10 billion in 1960 to almost $29 billion in 1970. Detailed breakdowns on the intergovernmental flows of funds are important but are too numerous for specific comment. Overall, the amounts show the magnitude of the links in 1970 between national, state, and local governments. The creative phase of IGR produced a highly interdependent, tightly bonded set of relationships. The IGR links were sometimes referred to as *"fused federalism,"* and it was said that "when national policy makers sneeze, the state and local ones catch pneumonia."

COMPETITIVE PHASE

The apparent tight links of the creative phase of IGR overstated reality. Even before the creative phase peaked (in dollar terms) at the end of the 1960s, there were signs of tension, disagreement, and dissatisfaction among many IGR participants, especially those at the state and local levels. Senator Edmund

Muskie perceptively pinpointed the nature of the tension. He had been a governor, and as a senator he chaired the Subcommittee on Intergovernmental Relations. As early as 1966 the senator observed, "The picture, then, is one of too much tension and conflict rather than coordination and cooperation all along the line of administration—from top federal policymakers and administrators to the state and local professional administrators and elected officials" [1; p. 62]. One example might be the case of a state health department head supporting provisions in national health legislation that differ from the policy position taken by his/her state's governor.

The tension and conflict to which Muskie referred between the "line of administration" and "professional administrators" laid bare a new type of fracture in IGR. This was the split between policy-making generalists, whether elected or appointed, and the professional program specialists. Figure 1 displays what ex-governor Terry Sanford (of North Carolina) called picket-fence federalism [6]. The metaphor illuminates the friction between the vertical functional allegiances of administrators to their specialized programs and the horizontal coordination intentions of the policy generalists—represented by the position-based associations of the "big seven" groups in Figure 1.

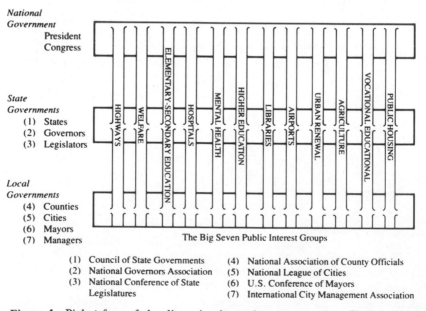

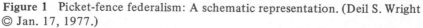

(1)	Council of State Governments	(4)	National Association of County Officials
(2)	National Governors Association	(5)	National League of Cities
(3)	National Conference of State Legislatures	(6)	U.S. Conference of Mayors
		(7)	International City Management Association

Figure 1   Picket-fence federalism: A schematic representation. (Deil S. Wright © Jan. 17, 1977.)

The "picket-fence" metaphor is an oversimplification in several respects [1, 7]. Nevertheless, it conveys some sense of the concerns and tensions present in IGR during the 1960s and early 1970s. Selective empirical research has shown the strong presence of specialized, functional attitudes among program administration officials [8].

The tolerance and support of the officials in the seven public interest groups had worn thin on behalf of categorical grant programs of both formula and project varieties. References were made to the "vertical functional autocracies," "balkanized bureaucracies," and the "management morass" that seemed associated with categorical forms of federal aid. The public interest groups shifted toward new policy stances, including support of general revenue sharing (enacted in 1972), broad-based block grants (several were passed), grant consolidations, and other similar proposals. A concise statement about the autonomous and fragmenting impacts of federal aid in the competitive IGR phase of the late 1960s and the 1970s came from a local official (in 1969) who observed that "our city is a battleground among warring Federal cabinet agencies" [9]. He was referring to the fact that various federal departments were funding, operating, and controlling "their" semiautonomous programs within the city.

CALCULATIVE PHASE

Previous discussion has pointed out that the time periods tied to each phase are imprecise and approximate. That point holds for the climax span of the current IGR phase—the calculative period. If forced to identify a precise data and event that signaled the rise of this phase, however, I would select 1975 and the event would be the near-bankruptcy of New York City. Telescoped into that episode, and into the continuing fiscal/social/economic plight of that city, were several issues that reflected some of the core problems of our society and our political system. Those problems range from accountability, bankruptcy, and constraints, to dependency, the federal role, and the loss of public confidence (see Table 1).

Main Problems

For years it had been difficult for New York City's citizens to identify and hold accountable those officials who were making major and costly public decisions [10-12]. For example, bond monies, ostensibly for capital construction, were used for equipment and even operating expenses. It finally took the private banking community, which was not without its share of blame for the malaise, to call a halt and push the city to the brink of bankruptcy. Constraints and severe cutback management were clamped on the city largely by national requirements connected with a temporary federal loan. The city also found

itself attempting to cope with other externally mandated and less yielding constraints—the three E's of economy (especially stagflation), energy, and environment.

New York City's route into, and thus far its provisional route through,
the crisis is illustrative of another common current problem in IGR—dependency.
And dependency is intimately attached to a larger problem: What is the appropriate role of the federal government? (As we shall see shortly, this issue has
reasserted itself in a manner and with a force that is reminiscent of the conflict
phase.) What are the boundaries and appropriate spheres within which the national government should (or should not) act? Finally, the problems of citizen
confidence or public trust in government(s) can likewise be discerned in the
New York City crisis.

New York City is a microcosm, albeit a large one, of an array of problems confronting our political system and its IGR dimensions. Fortunately,
most other jurisdictions have not suffered, and hopefully will not experience,
the convergence of such a problem-set. The significance and the dispersion of
the six problems mentioned above (see p. 21) across the nation are sufficient,
however, to demand attention and precautionary or preventive actions. Perhaps
the worst outlook or approach to adopt is to conclude that New York City's
plight is completely irrelevant to the difficulties, issues, and operations of other
governments—national, state, and local. Other entities and officials should avoid
the complacent attitude expressed in the famous (or infamous) phrase: "It
can't happen here!"

Participants' Perceptions and Behavior

What happened in IGR during the 1970s? What can be projected to extend well
into the 1980s? What are the current prominent perceptions of the main participants in IGR processes? Three chief perceptions are suggested as dominat-
ing the calculative phase. (There may well be others.) The three are fungibility,
gamesmanship, and overload. All three are tied directly to the characterization
of this phase as calculative.

The word *calculative* is used in at least three senses. First, it means to
think in advance of taking action, deliberating and weighing one or more avenues of action. A second meaning is to forecast or predict the consequences of
anticipated actions; it implies the adoption of a rather sophisticated, quasi-
scientific mode of thinking, perhaps best expressed in the form of the hypo-
thetical statement: "If . . ., then . . ." Third, calculative means to count, to figure, or to compute—in a numerical sense. In other words, quantitative forecast-
ing, usually measured in dollar units, is a prominent (but not universal) part of
the term's meaning. There are several types of behavior identifiable in contem-

porary IGR that are calculative in character, and these behavior patterns are expected to prevail in the near future.

One current calculative feature is the increased tendency to estimate the "costs" as well as the benefits of getting a federal grant. Two illustrations will suffice.

In 1976 the coordinator of state-federal relations for New York State reported that New York refused to pursue over $2 million in funds available to New York under the Developmental Disabilities Act. He notes that: "It would have cost us more than the two million we would receive to do the things that were required as a condition for receipt of the funds; my recommendation was not to take it and that was a hard one to make" [13]. Similarly at the local level, the city manager of a town with a population of 30,000 indicated (to the author) that unless a federal grant exceeded $40,000 he declined to inquire about or pursue it. Only a grant in excess of that "break-even" amount was sufficient to make it worth seeking. The calculation-based comment was made in 1973; subsequent inflation and increased federal regulations may have doubled that earlier threshold-seeking amount. It is clear from these illustrations that state and local administrators had become more cautious and calculative about their IGR fiscal efforts.

A second type of calculation involves the *formula game*. The formula game is the strategic process of attempting to change, in a favorable direction, one or more formulas by which federal funds are allocated among state and local governments. Increased attention to grant formulas has occurred since 1975 for two reasons. One is the widely heralded conflict between the snow belt and sun belt regions of the country. A second is that despite enactment of a large number of project grant programs, new as well as older formula grant programs account for nearly 80% of the $96 billion in estimated federal aid distributed in 1981.

An example of calculational strategy on a formula grant occurred with the extension of the Community Development Block Grant (CDBG) Program in 1977. The factors used in allocating $3.4 billion in 1978 CDBG funds were changed chiefly by substituting for "housing overcrowding" the "age of housing" (built prior to 1940) in a city. This formula revision heavily favored older industrial cities in the northeast and north central states at the expense of newer, younger, and smaller cities in southern and western states [14].

The stakes involved in calculative IGR can be huge. In any given year several formula grant programs totaling billions of dollars expire and must be reauthorized. It is easy to understand why experts, statistics, and computers have become commonplace in the present phase of IGR. A close observer of contemporary IGR captured the calculative propensities of this phase when he noted: "Public interest groups come into Washington with computer printouts with the [formula] weighting and what will happen if a certain weighting is approved" [15, 16].

Calculative behavior in three other areas of activity can be described in general terms. One involves coping with constraints and developing skills in cutback management. The International City Management Association, for example, has developed a program seminar with the title: "Managing with Declining Resources." The purpose of the sessions is to perfect operational techniques, quantitative and analytical, wherever possible, for making deliberate decisions on program reductions. Extensive attention has been devoted in the past few years to cutback management and coping with fiscal stress [17, 18].

A second example of calculation involves profits of $300 to $400 million that will accrue to several states from making federally subsidized loans to students attending colleges and technical schools. These profits, accumulating between 1980 to 1985, will be realized by the 18 states issuing student loan bonds plus the 10 other states that may do so for the first time in 1980 [19].

This situation occurs as a result of high interest rates, recent national tax and education legislation, and the active entry of several states, and even some local governments, into the student loan field. The profits will accrue to state (or local) governments in a manner that is best explained by two paragraphs from a Congressional Budget Office report. The report formally identified and calculated the estimated costs to the national government—and profit for the states.

> Student loan bonds are issued to provide students better access to loans. For a number of years, the federal government has induced commercial lenders to make student loans voluntarily, by offering them interest subsidies (a "special allowance") and insurance against student default. Even with these inducements, however, commercial lenders have been unwilling to lend to all student applicants because of the high cost of servicing student loans. As a result, some students have had trouble finding banks willing to lend to them, and an increasing number of states responded by issuing student loan bonds and then relending the proceeds to students.
>
> States and localities raise money by issuing bonds at low, tax-exempt interest rates and use the proceeds to buy or make federally guaranteed student loans at significantly higher interest rates, paid in large part by the federal government. Although the interest costs of nearly all student loan bond authorities were under 7 percent in 1979, for example, the yield they received on student loans fluctuated between 11 and 16 percent. The profits accruing to the bond issuers is the difference between the yield on student loans and the level of associated expenses—interest on the bonds and administrative costs. Lenders receive 7 percent interest paid by the

federal government until students leave school and by students thereafter. In addition, lenders receive special allowance payments from the federal government. The special allowance rate is recalculated each quarter and averaged 6.5 percent in 1979. [19; p. ix]

A final illustration of calculative behavior might best be summarized as the *risk* of noncompliance. This feature derives directly from the rising regulatory dimensions of IGR. A recent Office of Management and Budget (OMB) study identified 59 crosscutting or general national policy requirements [20]. These requirements are called *crosscutting* because they apply to the national assistance programs of more than one agency or department. In some cases they apply to *all* assistance programs in *every* department or agency, for example, nondiscrimination because of race, color, national origin, or handicapped status.

The significance and relevance of these requirements to the calculative phase of IGR are straightforward and twofold. One is the cost of compliance with the regulations by the recipients of federal assistance. Estimated costs of compliance with the equal access provisions for handicapped persons [21] in the public transportation field alone are estimated at $3 to $4 *billion*.

Recently a systematic study of local government compliance costs was conducted by Muller and Fix of the Urban Institute [22]. The researchers examined the incremental costs of complying with six major regulations in seven communities. The local units were Alexandria (Va.), Burlington (Vt.), Cincinnati, Dallas, Fairfax Co. (Va.), Newark, and Seattle. Among the regulations were bilingual education and transit accessibility for the handicapped. The study encompassed both capital and operating costs. The locally funded incremental costs varied from $6 per capita in Burlington to $52 per capita in Newark. The average across the seven units was $25 per capita. The authors set these compliance costs within the larger federal aid framework with the following observation: "One statistic can put the figures . . . into sharp perspective: the aid that the seven jurisdictions received under federal revenue sharing averaged about $25 per capita a year—essentially the same as what it cost them, on average, to comply with these regulatory programs" [22; p.31].

Another type of "cost" associated with these crosscutting requirements is one of noncompliance or, more accurately, incomplete compliance. It is hard to imagine any recipient of federal assistance that can fully comply with all the applicable policy requirements. The calculations laid on assistance recipients are ones that require tradeoffs or choices between these mandates, *provided* that the recipient is even aware of the applicability of a particular requirement. The OMB study described the forced choices and costs of the policy mandates and also allowed for the possibility that recipients might not know of some requirements because no one in the national government has been charged with knowing what they are.

> Individually, each crosscutting requirement may be sound. But cumulatively the conditions may be extraordinarily burdensome on federal agencies and recipients. They can distort the allocation of resources, as the conditions are frequently imposed with minimal judgement as to relative costs and benefits in any given transaction. Frequently, the recipients must absorb substantial portions of the costs. While the recipients may feel the full impact of these multiple requirements, there has been no one place in the federal government charged even with the task of knowing what all the crosscutting requirements are. [20; p. 20]

The 1970s as the starting period for the calculative phase of IGR is supported in part by temporal data on the 59 crosscutting requirements. About two-thirds of the socioeconomic policy requirements are a product of the 1970s. Over half of the administrative/fiscal requirements were placed in effect during the 1970s. Continuation of the calculative phase through the 1980s seems assured based on the likely permanence of this regulatory dimension of national assistance programs.

The remaining aspects of the calculative phase of IGR (see Table 1) deserve mention and brief exposition. The perceptions of participants are summarized with three terms—gamesmanship, fungibility, and overload. The first refers to the way in which participants in IGR processes engage in strategic behavior. They play various "games." Grantsmanship, for example, is one well-established game which, while identified with the creative phase, has been perfected through the competitive phase to the point that it is possible to specify some of the rules by which the grantsmanship game is played [23].

Fungible means interchangeable or substitutive. In intergovernmental terms fungibility means the ability to shift or exchange resources received for one purpose and accomplish another purpose. Several state governments will receive federal monies to subsidize student education loans. Those funds, once received by the states, are fungible after entering a state government's treasury and may be used for any purpose. General revenue sharing and block grant funds are noteworthy for their fungible or displacement effects. The receipt of such funds may permit the recipient unit to reduce the amount of its own resources devoted to the federally assisted program. The funds that are released from this substitution process can be allocated to other purposes or the process can result in a tax decrease.

An illustration of fungibility in connection with CETA funds in North Carolina is contained in Figure 2, "Fungible Funds from Federal Grants." CETA funds were used in 1975 to hire several hundred temporary employes by

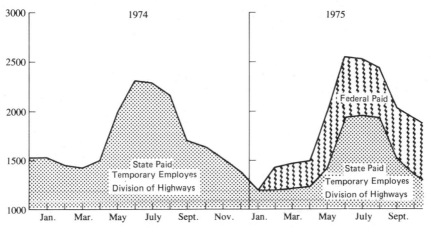

Temporary Highway Employment Month by Month in 1974 and 1975

Figure 2   Fungible funds from federal grants. (From *The News and Observer*, Raleigh, N.C., Sunday, Dec. 7, 1975.)

the Division of Highways. It was difficult to determine, however, how many of the federally funded positions were new jobs and how many were persons who were simply replacements in jobs that were previously state-funded. The average of state-paid jobs in 1974 was 1821 but dropped to 1532 in 1975. Peak state-paid employment in 1974 was about 2400; in 1975 it was below 2000.

Overload is a third dimension of participants' perspectives. The term gained considerable currency in the late 1970s, and it fits well the tone and temper of the calculative phase. A broader phrase, *political overload*, was used by James Douglas in 1976 to mean that "modern democratic governments [are] overwhelmed by the load of responsibilities they are called upon—or believe they are called upon—to shoulder" [24; p. 5]. Applied to the United States as a term criticizing governmental performance, the phrase has been interpreted to stand for excessive cost, ineffectiveness, and overregulation [24, 25]. These themes, when combined with the prior discussion of the crosscutting requirements, should adequately amplify the concept of overload.

A "weighty" example of overload recently surfaced at a New Jersey meeting attended by a staff member of the U.S. Regulatory Council (an interagency group that attempts to coordinate the 90 federal agencies issuing 2000 or more rules annually). Among the attendees was a mayor who had collected and weighed (literally) all the regulations and directives his city had received over the prior 18 months from different national and state agencies. The physical mass exceeded 2000 pounds [26]!

IGR Mechanisms and Metaphors

Several mechanisms are used to implement IGR activities in the calculative phase. One, as implied previously, is discretionary aid—general aid and block grants. These funds are dispensed on a formula basis. The legal term used in connection with the disbursements is indicative of a shift in participants' mindset about aid funds. The funds obtained by recipients are called *entitlements*. Jurisdictions are legally entitled to receive funding. This not only specifies the self-interest stake of the recipients; it escalates the possessive and proprietary *rights* of recipients. One consequence of these altered perspectives has been the rise of a new body of case law. One part of the large OMB study for *Managing Federal Assistance in the 1980s* identified nearly 500 court cases dealing with grants, and this was a "quick-and-dirty" effort to inventory the area [27] . A special conference held by the ACIR in late 1979 focused exclusively on the current status of grant law [28] . Explaining the sudden rise in grant-related cases (over three-fourths of the cases have originated since 1975), one conference participant observed that "the financial strains on state and local governments and the resultant paring down of available funds have brought about numerous lawsuits challenging the denial of grants or regulations which limit eligibility for grants" [29] . Shortly thereafter, the District of Columbia Bar sponsored a conference on "Federal Grant Litigation," with the candid subtitle: "Suing the Hand That Feeds You" [30] .

Associated with the mechanism of general aid is the technique of bypassing. Bypassing is the process of allocating federal monies directly to local governments without the funds passing through state government coffers. In 1960 only 8% of $7.2 billion, or $570 million, bypassed the states. This was an increase from $100 million in 1950. By 1970 about 16% of federal aid, or $3.5 *billion*, bypassed state governments. In 1980 about one-third of all federal aid went directly to local governments—approximately $30 billion.

Loans constitute a third implementing mechanism for IGR in the calculative phase. Many examples of loans in the IGR processes could be provided, two of which have been mentioned—to New York City and to students. The latter involved combined state and national financing participation with several states reaping handsome profits. Profit, however, was far from the mind of New York City officials during and after the bleak days of 1975.

The temporary federal loan in 1975 attached conditions which put the U.S. Secretary of the Treasury in the unique position of overseer of the city's financial operations and fiscal obligations. In statements and admonitions to city officials then Secretary William Simon called for reductions in expenditures, program cuts, management improvements, and so forth. But the Secretary also had several Simon-says mandates, for example, phasing out rent control and promptly implementing accounting and financial control systems. New York City's fiscal status remained in a near-crisis state for the remainder of the 1970s. It remained solvent only through the subsequent infusion of federal loans and grants. Yet the anomaly of a national cabinet official sitting in continuous oversight of the governance of New York City, or any other city, is no longer novel. It seems to be accepted as a normal state of affairs.

Regulation is the fourth and final implementing mechanism identified with the calculative phase. References to the *Federal Register*, crosscutting requirements, and grant law convey the prominence and significance of this subject. Perhaps the connecting point should be made with the participants' perceptions column. Without the *Federal Register* and the *Catalog of Federal Domestic Assistance*, it is difficult to become involved in IGR gamesmanship and grantsmanship. Furthermore, it is hazardous to engage in fungibility without an intimate knowledge of the assistance-related regulations associated with these and other documents. It is, however, difficult to cope with these mountainous materials without political and administrative overload. Therein lies the crux and the paradox of the calculative phase of IGR.

It is a phase that still contains many of the surface trappings of federalism. Local and state governments have the appearance of making significant policy choices. A few such choices may still remain, but they seem to be few and elusive. The chief choice that most nonnational participants have is deciding whether to participate in federal assistance programs. Once that choice is made, a large array of more limited choices appears open to those who have entered the federal assistance arena. A great deal of bargaining and negotiation takes place within that arena. But these are constrained chiefly, if not exclusively, by nationally specified rules of the game. That is why *facade federalism* is selected as the metaphor characterizing the calculative phase of IGR.

The term "facade" is used in both of its two usual meanings. First, it means the front or forward part of anything (usually a building). In this sense, the leading or frontal parts of governmental units' laws, structures, and officials are involved in the IGR exchanges. In other words, executives, legislative bodies, and courts are active and prominent participants. Associated with such involvement is the tendency toward confrontations, that is, face-to-face exchanges (such as court proceedings) that may or may not be amicably resolved.

Facade also means an artificial or false front. Dual aspects of this meaning are pertinent to the calculative phase of IGR. First, the false front put forth by some participants in intergovernmental exchanges may be contrived or artificial to bluff the other participants. Some IGR "games" played in the calculative phase may be like poker, a good bluff may win a "pot."

The other possible meaning of facade federalism is the absence or falseness of federalism. In other words, it could be argued that in some contemporary circumstances power has gravitated so heavily toward national officials that federalism, in its historical and legal sense, is nonexistent.

Whatever meaning is attached to facade federalism, it is clear that the 1980s will be a time in which the character and content of national-state-local relationships will continue to be debated and contested, refined and perhaps redefined. The nature and significance of the contests of refinements can be probed and understood, by student and practitioner alike, in minute events such as the making of student loans or in the passage of multibillion dollar aid programs, for example, the renewal of General Revenue Sharing.

CONCLUSION

One approach to understanding the contemporary character of intergovernmental relations is to see the present scene as the accretion of past patterns and relationships which fit a series of phases. These phases are analogous to layers of sedimentary rock in which the most evident is the current or surface layer. This present phase is called calculative, in part because of the emphasis on strategic or game-type behavior. This behavior has been encouraged, if not induced, by a startling array of events, problems, and difficulties that have confronted IGR participants and organizations.

Several elements of the calculative phase seem likely to persist through the 1980s. Indeed, the attitudes, actions, accomplishments, and proposals pursuant to the New Federalism of the Reagan administration seem destined to intensify calculative behavior among IGR participants. President Reagan's New Federalism is the fourth instance or variety of twentieth century policy initiatives designed to produce *new* departures in the arena of federalism and intergovernmental relations [31]. It may not be the last. But its four prominent thrusts of deconcentration, devolution, decrementalism, and deregulation appear likely to accentuate over the short run several of the patterns and perceptions of the calculative phase. To the extent that the current New Federalism is implemented, however, over the longer run it may produce a significant shift in intergovernmental patterns and result in yet another phase of IGR.

REFERENCES

1. Wright, Deil S. (1982). *Understanding Intergovernmental Relations*. Brooks/Cole, Monterey, California.
2. Elazar, Daniel J. (1962). *The American Partnership: Intergovernmental Cooperation in the Nineteenth Century*, University of Chicago Press, Chicago.
3. Grodzins, Morton (1966). *The American System: A New View of Governments in the United States*, (Daniel J. Elazar ed.)., Rand McNally, Chicago.
4. Bromage, Arthur W. (1943). Federal-state-local relations. *American Political Science Review 37*:35.

5. Mosher, Frederick (1968). *Democracy and the Public Service*, Oxford University Press, New York. See especially Ch. 4, "The Professional State."
6. Sanford, Terry (1967). *Storm Over the States*, McGraw Hill, New York.
7. Hale, George E., and Marian Lief Palley (1979). Federal grants to the states: who governs? *Administration and Society 11* (May):3-26.
8. Light, Alfred R. (1976). *Intergovernmental Relations and Program Innovation: The Institutionalized Perspectives of State Administrators*, Ph.D. Dissertation, University of North Carolina at Chapel Hill.
9. Sundquist, James, with David W. Davis (1969). *Making Federalism Work: A Study of Program Coordination at the Community Level*, Brookings Institution, Washington, D.C.
10. Sayre, Wallace, and Herbert Kaufman (1965). *Governing New York City*, Russell Sage Foundation, New York.
11. Caro, Robert A. (1974). *The Power Broker: Robert Moses and the Fall of New York*, Alfred A. Knopf, New York.
12. Auletta, Ken (1979). *The Streets Were Paved with Gold*, Random House, New York.
13. Greenblatt, Robert (1976). A comment on federal-state relations. In *Intergovernmental Administration: 1976- Eleven Academic and Practitioner Perspectives*, James D. Carroll and Richard W. Campbell, (eds.). Maxwell School of Citizenship and Public Affairs, Syracuse University, Syracuse, New York, pp. 143-171.
14. Adams, Jerome R., Thad L. Beyle, and Patricia J. Dusenbury (1979). The new "dual formula" for community development funds. *Popular Government 44*:33-37.
15. Walker, David B. (1979). Is there federalism in our future? *Public Management 61*:11.
16. Stanfield, Rochelle L. (1978). Playing computer politics with local aid formulas. *National Journal* (December 9):1977-1981.
17. Levine, Charles H. (1978). Organizational decline and cutback management. *Public Administration Review 38*:315-325.
18. Levine, Charles H. (1980). *Managing Fiscal Stress: The Crisis in the Public Sector*, Chatham House Publishers, Inc., Chatham, New Jersey.
19. Congressional Budget Office (1980). *State Profits on Tax-Exempt Student Loan Bonds: Analysis of Options*, CBO Background Paper, Washington, D.C.
20. Office of Management and Budget (1980). *Managing Federal Assistance in the 1980's*. Government Printing Office, Washington, D.C.
21. Sec. 504, Rehabilitation Act of 1973, P.L.93-112.
22. Muller, Thomas, and Michael Fix (1980). Federal solicitude and local costs: the impact of federal regulation on municipal finances. *Regulation 4*:29-36.
23. Wright, Deil S. (1980). Intergovernmental games: an approach to understanding intergovernmental relations. *Southern Review of Public Administration 3*:383-403.
24. Beer, Samuel H. (1977). Political overload and federalism. *Polity 10*:5-7.
25. Heclo, Hugh (1977). A question of priorities. *The Humanist 37*:21-24.
26. Petkas, Peter J. (1981). The U.S. regulatory system: partnership or maze? *National Civic Review 70*:297-301.

27. Office of Management and Budget (1979). *Managing Federal Assistance in the 1980's: Working Papers--(A-7)*, Survey of Case Law Relating to Federal Grant Programs, Executive Office of the President, Washington, D.C.

28. Advisory Commission on Intergovernmental Relations (ACIR) (1980). *Awakening the Slumbering Giant: Intergovernmental Relations and Federal Grant Law*, Government Printing Office, Washington, D.C.

29. *Public Administration Times* (1980). Aid Program Growth Spurs Rise of Grant Law, *3*:1.

30. Peters, Charles (1980). A way to control spending: FDR and Kennedy, and the games bureaucrats play. *The Washington Post*, April 25:F5.

31. Wright, Deil S. (1983). New federalism: recent varieties of an older species. *American Review of Public Administration* (forthcoming).

3
Changing Federal-Local Relations

George S. Blair Claremont Graduate School, Claremont, California

To paraphrase the words of an old song, both the American federal system and its subsystem of local governments "ain't what they used to be." Our nearly 2 centuries as a nation have witnessed major changes in both as well as changes in their interaction and relationships. Fortunately, space does not permit a long and detailed recital of specifics, but I will attempt to touch on briefly the highlights of recent changes and discuss the portents of the immediate future under President Reagan's New Federalism.

In typical definitions of American federalism, there is no mention of relationships between the national and local governments. This is because the theoretical foundations of our federal system are described rather than its actual operation. This dichotomy has been described discerningly to exist because "the theory of federalism has been characterized by rationalism, and the practice of federalism has been characterized by expediency" [1].

PERIODS OF AMERICAN FEDERALISM

While the national government has never been isolated from certain types of contact with local governments, they were largely negative in character until the early 1930s. In broad terms, we can divide the history of American federalism as it pertains to relationships between the national and local governments through 1980 into four distinguishable periods.

Dual Federalism (1790 to 1860)

This was a period of some squabbling between the nation and the states but generally a balanced period in which both levels grew steadily. It might be described in terms of railroad tracks—the two levels ran alongside each other, arguing occasionally as to which was the straighter, but they did not cross each other. Local governments were tightly controlled by the states in this period, and there were few relationships between them and the federal government. The exceptions were contacts with U.S. marshals in their pursuit of fugitives and for some internal improvement programs such as the loan of engineers and survey equipment by the central government to requesting local units.

Centralizing Federalism (1860 to 1930)

This was the period ushered in by the close of the Civil War and the Civil War amendments and was also the time national regulatory agencies began to be created and the federal income tax adopted. Local governments were even more tightly controlled by the states in the early part of this period but gained increasing freedom in the second half through the "home-rule" movement. Federal-local contacts, however, remained few in number and noncontinuous in nature. Limited programs of aid for local governments were funneled through the states with no direct federal-local fiscal relationships.

Cooperative Federalism (1930 to 1960)

The start of a basic change in the practice of American federalism was initiated with the advent of President Franklin Roosevelt's "New Deal" programs. The long tradition of funneling aid destined to local governments in the form of grants to the states for redistribution downward was shattered. Political scientist Roscoe Martin identified the year 1933 as a "geologic fault line" in the development of national-local relations [2]. Of the 132 categorical grant programs existing by 1960, however, only 15 were wholly of the direct federal-local type with no middleman role for the states [3]. The political theory of cooperative federalism continued to reflect an adherence to a strong dual federal relationship with very limited federal direct contact with local governments.

Cooptive Federalism (1960 to 1980) [4]*

This was the period of President Johnson's Great Society, Nixon's New Federalism, and Carter's New Partnership programs. Despite their many differences in goals and methods, these were all functional approaches stressing federal

*The term "cooptive federalism" is borrowed from Walker, Ref. 4.

government activism, intergovernmental cooperation, and complex linkages between and among the three levels. Great Society programs had a particular urban thrust and the former "50-50" allocation split of federal aid to urban and nonurban areas was changed to a "70-30" division favoring urban communities. While Nixon's New Federalism had a presumed federal-state bias, the general revenue sharing program and the two block grant programs in community development (CBDG) and the work force (CETA) resulted in an expansion of direct federal-local contacts and a further bypassing of the state. Carter's New Partnership was a curious blend of both Johnsonian and Nixonsonian tenets with a stress on improved intergovernmental procedures, fiscal conservatism, and programmatic flexibility [5].

The result of cooptive federalism was a cluster of developments in these 2 decades that transformed the three-tier intergovernmental system by a massive expansion of direct federal-to-local connections. The extent of this transformation is reflected in Table 1 which gives comparable data for selected years during this 20-year period. While all types of local government benefited from this expansion of direct federal aid, cities benefited the most [6].

STATUS AS OF 1980

There were two clear but contradictory trends during the 2 decades of cooptive federalism. The first was the rise of intergovernmental revenues to local governments and noncontinuing efforts to consolidate grant programs so that policy devolution could be furthered through block grants. The second trend was the growth of new forms of intergovernmental regulation.

Assessing developments of the 1960s, Sundquist wrote:

Table 1 Growth of Federal Aid to and Programs for State and Local Governments in Selected Years, 1960 to 1980

Year	Federal grants to state and local governments (in billions)	No. of categorical grant programs	Percentage of federal aid directly to local governments
1960	7.0	132	8
1969	20.3	341	12
1974	43.4	431	24
1977	68.4	492	28
1980	90.1	580	24

Source: Walker, David B. (September 5, 1981). The Changing Dynamics of Federal Aid to Cities. Paper presented at American Political Science Association Meeting, New York.

. . . The American federal system entered a new phase. Through a series of dramatic enactments, the Congress asserted the national interest and authority in a wide range of governmental functions that until then had been the province, exclusively or predominantly, of state and local governments. The new legislation not only established federal-state-local relations in entirely new fields of activity and on a vast scale but it established new patterns of relationships as well. [7]

This trend clearly continued through the decade of the 1970s, and many local officials felt trapped in the overlap of the contradictory thrusts. While the federal government increased its aid and decentralized some policy decisions on the one hand, this discretion seemed to fade with the rise of new federal regulation on the other hand. Thirty major statutes of intergovernmental regulation were enacted in the 15-year period from 1964 to 1978. These were:

1964 Civil Rights Act (Title VI)
1965 Highway Beautification Act
      Water Quality Act
1967 Wholesome Meat Act
1968 Civil Rights Act (Title VIII)
      Architectural Barriers
      Wholesome Poultry Products Act
1969 National Environmental Policy Act
1970 Occupational Safety and Health Act
      Clean Air Amendments
1972 Federal Water Pollution Control Act Amendments
      Equal Employment Opportunity Act
      Education Act Amendments (Title IX)
      Coastal Zone Management Act
1973 Flood Disaster Protection Act
      Rehabilitation Act (Section 504)
      Endangered Species Act
1974 Safe Drinking Water Act
      Hazardous Materials Transportation Act
      National Health Planning and Resources Development Act
      Emergency Highway Energy Conservation Act
      Family Educational Rights and Privacy Act
      Fair Labor Standards Act Amendment
1975 Education for All Handicapped Children Act
      Age Discrimination Act
1976 Resource Conservation and Recovery Act
1977 Surface Mining Control and Reclamation Act
1978 National Energy Conservation Policy Act
      Public Utility Regulatory Policy Act
      Natural Gas Policy Act [8]

While particular problems varied from program to program, the inter-governmental regulations resulted in a number of concerns to local officials. Seven frequent charges were that such regulations were (1) expensive, (2) inflexible, (3) inefficient, (4) inconsistent, (5) intrusive, (6) ineffective, and (7) unaccountable [9]. New York City Mayor Edward Koch estimated in 1980 that compliance with federal rules might cost that city as much as $7 billion over the next 4 years [10].

Federal regulation, of course, is not a recent development. Beam assesses recent regulatory forms in these words:

> What is quite new, and a sharp departure from traditional practices, is the growth of a host of federal regulatory programs *aimed at* or *implemented by* (emphasis in original) state and local governments. Beginning in the mid 1960s, and more notably during the 1970s, the federal regulatory presence has spilled over from the traditional economic sphere to include the nation's states, cities, school districts, colleges, and other public jurisdictions. What was quite unthinkable (and seemingly politically impossible) a few decades ago has both been thought of and come to pass. [8]

Beam identifies four major strategies in the new kit of techniques ro encourage acceptance of regulatory standards by local governments. These are (1) direct orders, (2) crosscutting requirements, (3) crossover sanctions, and (4) partial preemption (11). An example of a direct order is contained in the Equal Employment Opportunity Act of 1972 which bars job discrimination by local governments on the basis of race, color, religion, sex, and national origin. Crosscutting requirements are imposed on grants across the board to further national social and economic policies. For example, Title VI of the Civil Rights Act of 1964 stipulates that "no person in the United States shall, on the ground of race, color, or national origin, be excluded from participation in, be denied the benefits of, or be subjected to discrimination under any program receiving federal financial assistance." Crossover sanctions impose fiscal sanctions in one program area or activity to influence policy in another. The Emergency Highway Energy Conservation Act of 1974, for example, prohibits the approval of highway construction projects in states having a speed limit in excess of 55 miles per hour. Partial preemption rests on the authority of the federal government to mobilize local resources on behalf of national programs. Such a provision is a feature of the Clean Air Act Amendments of 1970.

Dubnick and Gitelson labeled partial preemption as "legal conscription", identifying it as

> ... an approach allowing national policymakers and policy implementors to mobilize state and local resources on behalf of a national program. As preliminary measures, these resources can be mobilized

using technical, financial, or other forms of assistance, but underlying this mechanism is the ability of national officials to formally and officially "draft" those resources into national service. [2]

In a study of constraint and opportunity for nine small California cities in our federal system, Sokolow and Snavely concluded that small town political leaders were receiving mixed signals from intergovernmental programs. They concluded:

> . . . On the one hand, the policy and procedural mandates which are imposed by higher governments tend to be seen as unnecessary restrictions on local governments. And if they suggest values foreign to the leadership of a small community, they may be opposed on ideological grounds. On the other hand, communities obviously benefit from the grant programs of higher governments, even though requirements are attached to the receipt of the aid. Few small communities lack a recognized set of public needs that can be met at least in part with federal and state aid, a fact apparent to their officials who increasingly engage in grantsmanship. [13]

By the end of the decade of the 1970s, however, the system of intergovernmental revenues and regulations had been diagnosed as seriously overloaded with congestion both at the center and at the periphery. According to David Walker, there were eight kinds of overload—judicial, fiscal, servicing, administrative, regulatory, political, intellectual, and philosophic [14]. Presidential candidate Ronald Reagan spoke out often about the overcentralized federal government and his intentions to curb its size and influence. The result of the 1980 election elevated him from candidate to incumbent and provided him with the opportunity to convert his goals into concrete policies.

One substantial change in intergovernmental relations, however, occurred in the waning days of the Carter administration. Congress finally approved reauthorization of General Revenue Sharing (GRS), first passed in 1972, renewed in 1976, and renewed again in 1980. But the 1981 renewal was for a 3-year period only and specified that local governments receive $4.6 billion in each of the next three fiscal years. Because of inflation, this continuing figure represents an actual cut in real terms, since the 1981 dollar purchases only two-thirds as much as the 1976 dollar—the year in which the $4.6 billion funding level was first reached. The 1981 renewal had one major difference; it excluded state governments from participation in the first year, and their inclusion in the subsequent 2 years is dependent upon the appropriations process. If states do receive their $2.3 billion in GRS funds in fiscal years 1982 and 1983, they must return to the federal treasury an equal amount of categorical grant funds [5]. While the GRS is no longer a strings-free program, it still allows greater flexibility to local officials than other federal programs, and its renewal was welcomed.

REAGAN'S NEW FEDERALISM

The tone of President Reagan's New Federalism was set forth clearly in his inaugural address. He stated:

> . . . It is my intention to curb the size and influence of the federal establishment and to demand recognition of the distinction between the powers granted to the federal government and those reserved to the states or to the people. All of us need to be reminded that the federal government did not create the states; the states created the federal government. [6]

By September, 1981, the direction of New Federalism had become substantially clear. It consisted of three major thrusts: (1) a dynamic economy with lower inflation, (2) devolution of power, programs, and funding to state and local governments, and (3) deregulation by major surgery on federal rules, regulations, and spending mandates that had been enacted in the previous 2 decades.

This "D to the third power" program received a mixed response from local officials. They welcomed the general goals and were hopeful, but they were equally apprehensive fearing that the road to their realization would be financially painful and necessitate service cutbacks and new local taxes. Local officials did not want to trade higher local taxes for reduced federal taxes, fearing the pains might well outweigh the gains and result in further citizen revolt at the polls. Many also feared the elimination and/or reduction in many federal programs they rely on to help their poorer citizens, their housing stock, and their capital improvement programs in such areas as sewers, airports, and mass transit. While the benefits would be real and were desired, they would be delayed in coming. The pains, on the other hand, would be immediate.

President Reagan's budget and tax packages were geared primarily to the first goal—a dynamic economy. Part of the massive budget cuts involved decreases in grants at about the 25% level for fiscal year 1982, no appropriation for at least 90 existing categorical programs, and the creation of seven block grant programs. As proposed by the president, 115 categorical aid programs would be consolidated into these seven block grants. Social services would combine 20 existing grants; health services, 22; preventive health services, 12; energy and energy assistance, 2; local special educational needs, 15; state programs for elementary and secondary education, 35; and community development, 9. Thus an important secondary impact of the budget proposals was to enhance the second goal—that of devolution of programs and activities [17].

While Congress responded favorably to Reagan's budget and tax packages in general, it did not approve his block grant proposals in full. Instead of the seven programs he requested, Congress approved nine. Instead of consolidating 115 existing categorical aid programs into these block grants, Congress consolidated 67, including 53 of those recommended by the president. The new block grants which did emerge from the legislative process were (1) community development (a miniblock to the states for nonentitlement local jurisdictions); (2) education, combining 34 categorical grants; (3) community services, consolidating six categorical grants; (4) health prevention and health services—seven categorical grants; (5) low-income energy and energy assistance —one categorical grant; (6) alcohol and drug abuse and mental health services— seven categorical grants; (7) primary care—one categorical grant; (8) maternal and child health care—one categorical grant; and (9) social services—two categorical grants.

Certain of these cuts and consolidations are of special significance to local officials. The two public service programs of CETA, which at one point had provided 725,000 jobs for low-income persons with long-term employment difficulties and persons out of work due to short-term fluctuations in the economy, were terminated at the end of fiscal 1981.

Housing programs were also impacted. President Carter's plan for 260,000 additional units of subsidized housing for FY 1982 was pared to 153,000 units. The low-income home ownership assistance program (Section 235) was phased out, and the rehabilitation loan program (Section 312), while extended through FY 1982, permitted loans only from the proceeds of the existing revolving loan fund—a figure far below the $129 million authorization for FY 1982 which was repealed.

The authorized $1 billion for economic development approved by Congress in 1980 for FY 1982 was reduced to $290 million. This extension further stipulated that no new projects may be approved that cannot be completed with the funds obligated in 1982.

Of the nine block grants, only the community development grant involves a continuing functional relationship for cities with the federal government. The other eight all go to the states with pass-through provisions for local governments in the block grant programs in education, community services, and primary care. The remaining five block grants call for a shift from federal-local to federal-state-local relationships. Chief local beneficiaries of these programs are counties, school districts, and nonprofit agencies—not the cities which fared better than other types of local government during the 2 decades of cooptive federalism.

Congressional action also provided for the specific elimination of appropriations for at least 20 other categorical programs for fiscal years 1982 to 1984.

While President Reagan did not achieve all the goals of the first phase of his program to streamline and simplify the grant-in-aid system, he was already making plans for the second phase. As reported in *The Washington Post*, he stated in early 1981 in an address before officials of the National Association of Counties that

> . . . I have a dream of my own. I think block grants are only the intermediate step. I dream of a day when the federal government can substitute for those, the turning back to local and state governments of the tax resources that we ourselves have preempted here at the federal level so that you would have the resources. [18]

Concerning the deregulation thrust, the new administration established a cabinet-level task force under the chairmanship of Vice President George Bush. In the spring months, this task force took 104 actions, with 34 of them providing relief to state and local governments. The task force will continue to meet and take administrative actions where appropriate, but a full scale deregulation effort must also involve both Congress and the courts.

The president's plan to decentralize the federal system is also the primary concern of two new advisory bodies. On April 8, 1981, Reagan announced the formation of a Presidential Federalism Advisory Committee under the chairmanship of Senator Paul Laxalt of Nevada, and he earlier established a 12-member Task Force to undertake a similar program.

Senator Laxalt is also chairman of the Task Force, which includes such top White House aides as Chief of Staff James Baker, Edwin Meese, Martin Anderson, and Robert Carlson; Intergovernmental Relations Assistant Richard Williamson; five cabinet members; and OMB Director David Stockman.

In addition to the 12 Task Force members, the Presidential Federalism Advisory Committee includes 40 representatives drawn from Congress, state government, local government, and private citizens. The committee is charged with providing the president with information on the effects of federal policies on states and local governments, with advising the administration on methods and means to implement its proposals, and with developing long-term policies to reverse the centralization of program control in Washington. The committee held its first meeting on June 23 of 1981. While this was largely an organizational and get-acquainted meeting, it was clear that its members are far from united on how it should or could achieve its assignment.

Not to be outdone, Congress also moved to bring issues of federalism before it by proposing the creation of a Commission for More Effective Government. The task of this commission would be twofold—to examine the federal government and find ways to improve its organization and operations and to study the federal system and recommend ways to improve relationships among the three levels of government.

Plans for further deep budget cuts were under consideration in mid-

September. Local officials were alarmed at the rumored possibility that General Revenue Sharing would be cut back by $500 million in 1983 and phased out over a three-year period. Other potential programs for cutback recommendations were community development grants, public housing programs, mass transit, and the energy support program to help low-income persons pay their their heating bills [19].

CONCLUSION

It is too early to describe all of the features of President Reagan's New Federalism and their impact on local governments. Stanfield drew an interesting analogy by comparing federal-state relations to the old folk tale about two brothers who decided to buy a cow and share it half-and-half. The younger brother got the front half which he had to feed, while the older brother picked the back half from which he got milk. Stanfield reminds us that the brothers should have divided responsibilities so that the cow gets fed and milked at regular intervals. If the younger brother can't afford to or is too lazy to feed the cow, it won't give milk and might even die. If that should happen, the older brother has few viable options [20].

The analogy holds equally true for federal-local relations. The cuts in federal aid are real and are being felt in communities across the nation. One interesting and likely possibility has been suggested by Peirce. He foresees that budget economies and the New Federalism agenda "will force normally quarrelsome state and city governments to smoke a peace pipe—or conceivably even form a new alliance in dealing with Washington" [21].

One step in this direction was taken by the National Governors Association at its annual meeting in August, 1981 when a panel of mayors and county officials was invited to participate. The association created a new permanent Committee on State-Local Relations to build "strong bridges to our counties, cities, towns, and school districts."

At least for the duration of New Federalism, it seems certain that the pattern of interdependency between local governments and the national center will be declining, while the interdependency between states and their local governments will be increasing. The focus of New Federalism on the federal system provides a unique opportunity for its reform. There is near unanimity that reform is needed, but the chorus of chanting voices is far from unison in the particulars of that reform.

REFERENCES

1. Burkhead, Jesse, and Jerry Minor (1971). *Public Expenditures*, Aldine-Atherton, New York, p. 254.

2. Martin, Roscoe C. (1965). *The Cities and the Federal System*, Atherton Press, New York, p. 111.

3. Walker, David B. (September 5, 1981). The Changing Dynamics of Federal Aid to Cities. Paper presented at American Political Science Association, New York, p. 1.

4. Walker, David B. (1981). *Toward a Functioning Federalism*, Winthrop Publishers, Inc., Cambridge, Mass., p. 16.

5. Walker, David B. (1981). *Toward a Functioning Federalism*, Winthrop Publishers, Inc., Cambridge, Mass., pp. 116-122.

6. Advisory Commission on Intergovernmental Relations (July 1980). *Recent Trends in Federal and State Aid to Local Governments*, M-118, Washington, D.C., pp. 42-51.

7. Sundquist, James L. (1969). *Making Federalism Work: A Study of Program Coordination at the Community Level*, The Brookings Institution, Washington, D.C., p. 1.

8. Beam, David R. (Summer 1981). Washington's regulation of states and localities: origins and issues. *Intergovernmental Perspective 7*:8-18 p. 9.

9. Beam, David R. (Summer 1981). Washington's regulation of states and localities: origins and issues. *Intergovernmental Perspective 7*:8-18 p. 13.

10. Muller, Thomas, and Fix, Michael (Spring 1981). Federal rules, local costs. The Urban Institute, *Policy and Research Report 11*:1-3.

11. Beam, David R. (Summer 1981). Washington's regulation of states and localities: origins and issues. *Intergovernmental Perspective 7*:8-18, p. 10.

12. Dubnick, Mel, and Gitelson, Alan (1981). Nationalizing state policies. In *The Nationalization of State Government*, Hanus, Jerome J. (ed.). D. C. Heath and Company, Lexington, Mass., pp. 56-57.

13. Sokolow, Alan, and Snavely, Keith (March 26-28, 1981). Constraint and Opportunity for Small Cities in the Federal System, Paper presented at Western Political Science Association, Denver, p. 1.

14. Walker, David B. (1981). *Toward a Functioning Federalism*, Winthrop Publishers, Inc., Cambridge, Mass., pp. 251-255.

15. Mitchell, Michael C. (Winter 1981). Washington grapples with the budget crunch, *Intergovernmental Perspective 7*:8-18, p. 10.

16. *Los Angeles Times*, January 21, 1981, p. 16.

17. This paragraph and the ones which follow assessing the early emphasis and impact of President Reagan's New Federalism are based generally on information and data provided in Walker, David B. (1981). The Changing Dynamics of Federal Aid to Cities. Paper presented at American Political Science Association, New York, pp. 8-13.

18. *Intergovernmental Perspective 7* (Spring 1981):4.

19. *Los Angeles Times*, September 19, 1981, pp. 1, 24.

20. Stanfield, Rochelle L. (August 29, 1981). The dry end of the deal. *National Journal 13*:1554.

21. Peirce, Neal R. (September 1, 1981). Federalism forges unlikely alliance. *Public Administration Times 4*:2, 10.

4
Interjudicial Relations

John W. Winkle III   University of Mississippi, University, Mississippi

Parallel judicial power is a basic feature of American federalism. The dynamics of our dual court system, however, remain largely unexplored in the literature of political science [1-3]. Recent studies that do address this theme are found mainly in legal periodicals and for the most part are limited to investigations of Supreme Court rulings that affect jurisdictional prerogatives [4, 5]. Yet the linkages between state and federal courts and judges are also important to political analysts. Within the context of interjudicial relations, for example, old and vital concerns such as the allocation of authority, administration of justice, litigant behavior, and public policymaking emerge in a new light. The purpose of this chapter is several-fold: to refine the frameworks for analysis of interjudicial relations; to introduce a dimension that focuses on the interaction of judges, not courts; and to sketch future implications in light of contemporary patterns.

The distinction between federalism and intergovernmental relations (IGR) is a useful point of departure for this discussion [6]. Conventional definitions of federalism include, among other features, its static character and its legalistic division of authority and functions between states and nation. On the other hand, IGR emphasizes regular and informal interactions of public officials at national, state, and local levels. It stresses, moreover, process not

This is a revision of a paper presented at the 1980 Annual Meeting of the Southern Political Science Association, Atlanta, Georgia, November 6-8, 1980.

structure, policy not law, and change not constancy. The following discussion explores the extent to which these distinctions are appropriate for the analysis of interjudicial relations.

JUDICIAL FEDERALISM

Judicial federalism describes the general framework within which interjudicial relations take place. It sets forth the structure and intersystem rules. The division of authority between state and federal courts for the most part is prescribed by the Constitution, Congressional statutes, and Supreme Court decisions. Naturally, this gives judicial federalism a fixed, but not rigid, legalistic demeanor.

Judicial federalism, it seems, may be approached from two distinct perspectives. At the heart of both models are two fundamental questions. First, to what extent are state courts sensitive to federal constitutional norms? And, second, are state judges competent to protect and uphold those norms [7]? When state judiciaries are seen as insensitive and incompetent, the intersystem relationship is characterized by rivalry and conflict. Conversely, when state courts are perceived as solicitous and capable of safeguarding federal rights, the relationship assumes an accommodating, even deferential, character. It is appropriate now to describe further each model of judicial federalism and then place them into some historical perspective.

The Conflict Model

Parallel judicial systems with overlapping jurisdiction invite conflict. The American experience is no exception. Discord between state and federal courts has historically focused on diversity of citizenship jurisdiction, federal common law doctrines, preemption, habeas corpus relief, removal formulas, and injunctions. All of these friction points, of course, involve the exercise of federal powers of legal and equitable relief. Underlying them are the acknowledged supremacy of federal law and the presumed superiority of federal justice. Present as well is the perceived inadequacy of state remedies.

Clearly, judicial federalism is assymetrical. Federal courts in theory have significant authority to intervene before, during, and after state proceedings in order to protect federally guaranteed rights. Needless to say, perhaps, these actions may threaten state court autonomy. On the other hand, state judiciaries enjoy no such reciprocity [8]. Thus this model accents disparities and creates a superior-subordinate hierarchy. Not surprisingly, therefore, this arrangement has led to rivalry and disruption.

The conflict model does not necessarily impute intent, namely, that federal courts aggressively seek opportunities to antagonize states. Because of statutory directives, federal courts at times cannot deny their jurisdiction even if they so choose, as in diversity suits. And, on occasions especially in the nineteenth century, state courts defiantly triggered conflict [9]. Regardless of motivation, an uneasy interplay between institutions continues under this model of judicial federalism.

The Deference Model

Not all relations between state and federal courts are abrasive. Devices fashioned mainly by judges themselves attempt to mitigate the inherent frictions of judicial federalism. At the heart of these self-imposed restraints is a conscious desire to preserve the integrity of state court proceedings. This model sees state tribunals as competent partners. It assumes some degree of parity.

Among the more common deferential devices are comity, abstention, exhaustion of remedies, and certification. A lengthy explanation is unnecessary here but some basic comments are appropriate. Comity, a principle "of right and of law, and therefore of necessity" [10], urges restraint in order to avoid unwanted collisions of authority. Abstention, popularized some 40 years ago [11, 12], allows federal courts to postpone decisions pending state interpretation. The exhaustion of remedies rule, spelled out by both statutory and decisional law, requires petitioners to seek appropriate state relief before turning to federal forums. Finally, certification of troublesome questions by federal courts to state courts of last resort provides a further opportunity for deference. These strategems share a common objective of reducing intersystem rivalry by limiting access to, or action by, federal courts. All, however, suffer to varying degrees from imprecise guidelines and selective application.

With a general image of these models in mind, it is useful now to put them into some historical perspective. The following discussion is a synopsis of state and federal court relations over 2 centuries. As such, it risks grave oversimplification and probably understates the complexity of the relationship. The illustrations and patterns, however, are representative. No attempt is made to develop rigid time frames, a rather impossible task except perhaps in recent decades.

Conflict and Deference in Historical Perspective

Almost without exception, delegates to the Philadelphia Convention of 1787 agreed upon the need for a national supreme court [13, 14]. What they questioned, however, was the desirability of an accompanying federal subsystem. Floor debates revealed two opposing fears: federal encroachment versus state partisanship. An eventual compromise postponed the creation of lower federal courts but Article III authorized Congress "from time to time to ordain and establish tribunals inferior to the Supreme Court." When Congress set up a national subsystem in the Judiciary Act of 1789 [15], it nonetheless deferred greatly to state adjudication. The newly created district and circuit courts were saddled with severe jurisdictional constraints [16]*. State tribunals, in fact, served for years as courts of first instance even in federal matters.

A gradual redistribution of judicial power occurred during the nineteenth century, however, and the once preeminent posture of state adjudication deteriorated. Both the federal courts and Congress showed, in general, increasingly less deferential attitudes. The Marshall Court, for example, in a series of landmark decisions underscored the supremacy of federal law and courts [18-21]. Even during the Taney era, long noted for its states rights tendencies, federal courts fared well. In *Swift* v. *Tyson* (1842), for example, the Supreme Court ruled that federal judges must apply state statutory, but not decisional, law [22]. Not long afterward, the Court denied Wisconsin judges the privilege of releasing prisoners in federal custody through the writ of habeas corpus. In one such case, Justice Field asserted that only the national government could "intrude with its judicial process into the domain" on the state in order to "preserve its rightful supremacy" [23]. Congress increased diversity jurisdiction, expanded federal habeas corpus relief to include persons in state custody [24], and, in 1875, gave federal question jurisdiction to U. S. District Courts [25].

The twentieth century has witnessed a vacillation between the conflict and deference models. The first 50 years found federal courts honoring with some regularity the principles of comity and abstention[26]. And the Supreme Court in *Erie* v. *Tompkins* (1938) discarded the troublesome *Swift* precedent [27]. But that deference soon encountered stiff resistance from the Warren Court (1953 to 1969) and its emphasis on national protection of individual and group rights. Desegregation and reapportionment formulas [28, 29], preemption doctrines [30], removal options [31], and liberalized habeas corpus procedures [32, 33], all enhanced federal judicial power at the expense of state courts and legislatures. The need to secure national norms outweighed concerns for state diversity or autonomy.

Actions by the Burger Court, however, reflect a growing concern for federal workloads and for state processes. The watershed in this "jurisdictional counter-revolution" [34, 35] was *Younger* v. *Harris* in 1971 [36]†. Under the

---

*See also the anti-injunction statute, Ref. 17. Judge-made exceptions, however, eventually arose.

†State court prejudice, however, is still grounds for issuing an injunction. See Ref. 37.

emblem of "our federalism," the court announced that only in extraordinary circumstances may federal courts enjoin state criminal proceedings [38]*. Three years later, *Lehman Brothers* v. *Schein* [39] underscored the use of the certification process. The court has also systematically restricted access to federal forums. *Stone* v. *Powell* (1976), for example, held that federal habeas corpus is unavailable for petitioners who have been provided full and fair opportunities to litigate Fourth Amendment claims in state courts [40, 41]. Noninterference, it seems, has become an unmistakable norm [42, 43]†.

Certain factual and normative inquiries are deliberately placed beyond the scope of this paper. Do state courts deserve federal respect? Have federal courts abdicated responsibility? Should national rights be preserved even at severe costs to intersystem harmony? What values are most important in a federal system? While these are vital questions, the immediate purpose of this chapter is to present frameworks for the analysis of interjudicial relations. And the totality of those relations cannot be explained by the judicial federalism approach alone. The interplay of individual actors is a significant theme of this drama.

INTERACTION OF JUDGES

Judges from the two systems interact just as other officials do. While studies have examined the behavior of state and federal judges at trial and appellate levels, none has systematically investigated patterns of intersystem exchange. Important in and of itself, this intergovernmental dimension may provide a useful guide in understanding trends in judicial federalism.

From the outset it must be admitted that relations between judges do not fit tightly into common perceptions of IGR. The reasons are evident. As the discussion of judicial federalism indicated, judges operate in an environment constrained by jurisdictional rules and legal norms. As a result, they enjoy somewhat less flexibility and maneuverability than other public officials. Unlike IGR, moreover, a multiple unit relationship (nation, state, local) may not neatly exist here. But regular, informal, and varied interactions do occur with surprising frequency.

The nature and scope of this relationship is difficult to determine primarily because of a fundamental lack of information. A historical analysis is practically impossible. While interaction between state and federal judges

*Justice Black in his majority opinion describes "our federalism" as the "belief the National Government will fare best if the states and their institutions are left free to perform separate functions in their separate ways."
†Ref. 43 corroborates the view held in Ref. 42.

undoubtedly has occurred over time in the course of performing judicial business, the best guess is that exchange was sporadic. It is altogether plausible that professional relationships reflected the conflict-deference characteristics of the above models, but this is difficult to prove. Some observations, however, are possible.

For the most part, there have been no ongoing vehicles to stimulate intersystem contact. Committees and councils of judges in each system have independently discussed issues that touch upon the federal-state relationship. Until recently, however, no joint ventures took place. Judges from one system have on occasion attended meetings or conferences sponsored by the other as special guests or speakers. Annual state bar association meetings also provided opportunities for exchange. Whether these sessions alone qualify under the IGR perspective is debatable.

The Modern Perspective

Judicial interaction today is promoted by institutional and associational mechanisms. Each court stystem, for example, maintains a national headquarters that is increasingly involved with interjudicial matters. The Federal Judicial Center, established in 1967, has provided research and advisory assistance to state judges. It continues to sponsor intersystem programs and seminars and maintains strong liaison with state judicial associations. Its monthly bulletin, *The Third Branch*, runs a column on "State-Federal News." In addition, the center has collaborated with the National Center for State Courts (created in 1971) on special projects.

Professional organizations in recent years have also recognized the need for intersystem cooperation. The Judicial Conference of the United States, the Conference of Chief Justices, the American Bar Association, and the American Judicature Society have all to varying degrees supported that goal [44]. Moreover, an Appellate Judges Conference with representatives from both systems has been created with a possible trial court association to follow [45]. These associational and institutional linkages, however, do not embrace all relations between and among judges as the discussion will show.

The following discussion is based largely on data secured through a questionnaire survey of state chief justices in 1979. Subsequent telephone interviews resulted in the participation of all 50 states. The survey instrument aimed specifically at state-federal judicial councils and generally at intersystem relations.

The Councils

Ten years ago, Chief Justice Warren Burger recommended the creation of a state-federal judicial council in each state "to maintain continuous communication on all joint problems" [46]. State and federal judges would meet together to identify common concerns, outline objectives, and work toward intersystem cooperation. By mid-1972, more than 30 councils had been set up with others planned [47]*. Established through court orders, these bodies enjoyed neither legislative funding nor staff. While only nine remain vitally active today†, survey responses suggest that the joint councils made a positive contribution to state-federal relations. One judge commented that the "mere existence" of a council "promoted the harmony which is desired."

Not all states set up joint councils‡. Almost without exception, chief justices in those jurisdictions reported "no need for such an organization." Judges "visited informally several times a year," they claimed, and sometimes settled problems by telephone. Chief justices in states with inactive councils echoed those sentiments as well. Intergovernmental contact occurs with some frequency even without joint councils.

Judges from trial and appellate levels constituted 92% of the total membership of councils§. Recruitment at organizational meetings was highly informal with state chief justices and federal chief judges by and large accepting volunteers. State representatives slightly outnumbered federal. Nonjudicial personnel accounted for the remaining 8%. Most of these delegates—attorneys general, bar association appointees, consultants, court administrators, and law professors—came from the state level and were concentrated in a few geographically scattered councils.

Actual contact between officials is important to IGR. Most councils convened semiannually or annually, usually at prearranged events such as federal circuit conferences or bar association conventions. These meetings permitted judges "to become better acquainted," the first step in building intersystem bridges. Regular sessions stimulated a "continuing dialogue," one chief justice wrote, which "benefits the two systems, the public, and the litigants."

---

*The Federal Judicial Center reported that 35 states had created councils and 8 more would probably follow suit.

†The nine states with active councils in 1981 were: Arkansas, Georgia, Maine, Minnesota, Mississippi, Missouri, Oregon, Washington, and Wisconsin.

‡Ten states that did not establish councils are: Massachusetts, North Carolina, North Dakota, Rhode Island, South Carolina, South Dakota, Tennessee, Utah, West Virginia, and Wyoming.

§Appellate judges represented 61% of the state judicial component and 29% of the federal.

These councils served as sounding boards for judicial expression and seemingly sensitized judges to the respective rights and responsibilities of the two systems. The interchange led to "mutual respect" and "made more realistic and effective" the "professional relationship." Once regular communication developed, "other important areas of common concern surface[d]" [48]. One chief justice remarked that the council had stimulated "better understanding . . . and the birth of good ideas."

Since 1970, councils have addressed a broad range of topics and have brought about some intersystem changes. Survey responses indicate that judges considered legalistic-jurisidctional matters more significant than administrative ones. Longstanding sorespots, such as state prisoner petitions and diversity litigation, appeared regularly on council agendas and were the subject of special seminars and workshops sponsored by councils. Administrative concerns centered mostly on court management issues: among others, calendar conflicts, selection of jurors, sharing resources, and rule-making authority. The councils have achieved modest success, mainly in the expedition of cases and the elimination of duplicative procedures. No one could expect much more in the way of substantive reform from ad hoc bodies, operating under major support constraints.

The primary purpose of this section is to introduce a new way of viewing interjudicial relations, not to scrutinize the achievements of councils. Their contributions do show, however, that interaction between judges is neither insignificant nor aimless. Just what impact, if any, these contacts may have on the conflict-deference dimension of judicial federalism is difficult to say. That judges in this context, however, could influence policy and programs even in limited ways is significant for IGR.

THE FUTURE

What does the future hold for interjudicial relations? Will judicial federalism continue to reflect the patterns of dominance and deference? Will the interaction of state and federal judges influence the distribution of judicial power? Will the relationship take new and unexpected turns? What factors will moderate the pace and direction of intersystem relations? Several scenarios drawn from the axis of constancy and change are possible. Some are less likely than others if one uses as a qualified guide the American historical and political experience. Because change in our system occurs gradually, not suddenly, drastic changes, while possible, are probably unrealistic. It seems that three scenarios offer the most plausible views of future interjudicial relations.

The First Scenario

If present patterns of interaction persist, the immediate future is clear. Despite the historical dominance of the conflict model, modern judicial federalism is now within a period of deference. The Supreme Court, a principal factor in any future scenario, currently shows strong tendencies in that direction. Inter-system harmony is, as Justice Powell suggested in his majority opinion in *Stone* v. *Powell*, *supra*, an important value in judicial decision making. The ability of state courts to handle well their newly gained responsibility is a critical, but manageable, factor in maintaining federal trust. The routine interaction of state and federal judges, moreover, echoes the theme of cooperation. Tensions, whether real or imagined, have lessened. Relations between judges "are in much better state of affairs than they were just ten or a dozen years ago" [49] . Informal communications will likely continue despite the growing inactivity of joint councils. Those mechanisms still exist if future needs arise.

The Second Scenario

Deference may be short-lived. It is altogether possible that there will be a return to the conflict dimensions of the Warren era. Some analysts find alarming the solicitude of the Burger Court toward state interest [50] . What they fear is that federal rights will go unprotected or that those liberties will be severely impaired. State institutions are neither as vigilant nor as responsive as federal forums, they claim. Until states improve both the availability and adequacy of their own remedies, federal intervention is mandatory. If these charges prove accurate, Congress and the Supreme Court (with or without changes in personnel) may reactivate national power, which in turn may escalate intersystem tensions. Adding to this scenario is the fact that relations between judges may not remain positive. Because of the declining use of joint councils, for example, judges do not engage as frequently in purposive problem solving. Nor are jurisdictional and administrative problems between the two court systems gone. Coupled with probable turnover of judges at both levels in the next few years, there may be significant interruptions in the present patterns of behavior.

The Third Scenario

Interjudicial relations may neither remain static nor move toward conflict. Instead, there may occur a virtual merger of the two court systems. The view is not preposterous. Even Chief Justice Burger expressed concern over this possibity in his 1980 address to the American Law Institute [52] . At least one respected scholar has recently identified signals that may point toward convergence [53]. States are increasingly moving toward adoption of uniform rules of procedure (and perhaps evidence) similar, if not identical, to federal standards. Growing associational ties between state and federal judges may to some degree encourage uniform thinking as well. Congress, moveover, has been investing millions of dollars annually in state court improvement projects and research. While the Law Enforcement Assistance Administration (the principal national benefactor of state courts) is now defunct, there is some reason to expect there will not be a reduction in allocations. The proposed State Justice Institute would require a substantial outlay of federal funds. This financial linkage is significant because some intriguing questions arise. Would Congress ever impose federal standards upon state courts in return for money? If so, would dependent states comply with such eligibility requirements? Quasi-merger looms as a future alternative.

CONCLUSION

Which of these futures, if any, is probable or preferable is difficult, if not impossible, to say. About all that can be offered at this time are unsatisfying generalizations. Jurisdictional tensions, to varying degrees, will always exist in our federal system. And their presence is not wholly undesirable. By the same token, effort to accommodate national and state interests will, in all likelihood, continue as well.

Regardless of which scenario prevails, interjudicial relations and issues will influence court administration in the 1980s. As in other intergovernmental arenas, ever-increasing demands to streamline management, preserve scarce resources, and upgrade delivery of services also face state and federal courts. The ongoing pressures of judicial federalism cannot help but accent these concerns. If court management is to become more effective and efficient, judges, administrators and legislators alike must give serious attention to inter-system linkages. The nature and scope of interjudicial relations, it seems, will likely remain an important topic for inquiry and refinement in the decade ahead.

REFERENCES

1. Cole, Kenneth (October 1942). *Erie* v. *Tompkins* and the relationship between federal and state courts. *American Political Science Review 36*: 885-895.
2. Wendell, Mitchell (1949). *Relations Between Federal and State Courts*. Columbia University Press. New York.

3. Winkle, John W. (November 1974). Dimensions of judicial federalism. *The Annals of the American Academy of Political and Social Science* *416*:67-76.

4. McGowan, Carl (Spring 1978). Federal jurisdiction: legislative and judicial change. *Case Western Reserve Law Review 28*:517-555.

5. Weinberg, Louise (July 1977). The new judicial federalism. *Stanford Law Review 29*:1191-1244.

6. This discussion is based on Wright, Deil (1978). *Understanding Intergovernmental Relations*, Duxbury Press, North Scituate, Mass., pp. 16-19.

7. Rosenfeld, Stephen S. (1979). Stimulus-response federalism: the relation between supreme court deference and state court justice. In *The Courts: The Pendulum of Federalism*. The Roscoe Pound-American Trial Lawyers Foundation, Washington, D.C., pp. 113-137.

8. *McKim* v. *Voorhies*, (1812). 11 U.S. 279.

9. Warren, Charles (1930). Federal and state court interference. *Harvard Law Review 43*:345-378.

10. *Covell* v. *Heyman*, (1884). 111 U.S. 176, 182.

11. *Railroad Commission* v. *Pullman*, (1941). 312 U.S. 496.

12. *Burford* v. *Sun Oil Co.*, (1943). 319 U.S. 315.

13. Farrand, Max, ed. (1911). *The Records of the Federal Convention of 1787*, Yale University Press, New Haven, p. 1.

14. Frank, John P. (Winter 1948). Historical bases of the federal judicial system. *Law and Contemporary Problems 13*:3-28.

15. Judiciary Act of September 24, 1789, 1 Stat. 73.

16. Redish, Martin H. (1980). *Federal Jurisdiction: Tensions in the Allocation of Judicial Power*, Bobbs-Merrill, Indianapolis, p. 259.

17. Act of March 2, 1783, 1 Stat. 334.

18. *Marbury* v. *Madison*, (1803), 1 Cranch 137.

19. *Martin* v. *Hunter's Lessee*, (1816), 14 U.S. 304.

20. *Cohens* v. *Virginia*, (1821), 19 U.S. 264.

21. *Gibbons* v. *Ogden*, (1824), 9 Wheat, 1.

22. *Swift* v. *Tyson* (1842), 41 U.S. 1.

23. *Tarble's Case*, (1872), 80 U.S. 397, 407.

24. Act of February 5, 1867, 14 Stat. 385.

25. Act of March 3, 1875, 13 Stat. 470.

26. Compare *Ex parte Young*, (1908) 209 U.S. 123 with *Ponzi* v. *Fessenden*, (1922), 258 U.S. 254.

27. *Erie* v. *Tompkins* (1938), 304 U.S. 64.

28. *Brown* v. *Board of Education*, (1955), 349 U.S. 294.

29. *Reynolds* v. *Sims*, (1964), 377 U.S. 533.

30. *Pennsylvania* v. *Nelson*, (1956), 350 U.S. 497.

31. Johnson, Harvey M. (Spring 1966). Removal of civil rights cases from state to federal courts: the matrix of section 1443. *Federal Bar Journal 26*:99-155.

32. *Townsend* v. *Sain*, (1963), 372 U.S. 293.

33. *Fay* v. *Noia*, (1963), 372 U.S. 391.

34. Weinberg, Louise (July 1977). New judicial federalism. *Stanford Law Review 29*:1203. Cf. Ref. 35.

35. Walker, David B. (1981). *Toward a Functioning Federalism*, Winthrop, Cambridge, Mass., pp. 139-140.

36. *Younger* v. *Harris* (1971), 401 U.S. 37.

37. *Gibson* v. *Berryhill*, (1973), 411 U.S. 564.

38. 401 U.S. 37, 44 (1971).

39. *Lehman Brothers* v. *Schein* (1974), 416 U.S. 385.

40. *Stone* v. *Powell* (1976), 428 U.S. 465.

41. *Wainwright* v. *Sykes* (1977), 433 U.S. 72.

42. Howard, A. E. Dick (1979). The supreme court and federalism. In *The Courts: The Pendulum of Federalism*. The Roscoe Pound-American Trial Lawyers Foundation, Washington, D.C., p. 60.

43. *Moore* v. *Sims*, (1979), 442 U.S. 415.

44. Glendening, Parris N., and Mavis Mann Reeves (1977). *Pragmatic Federalism*. Palisades Publishers, Pacific Palisades, Calif., p. 59.

45. *The Third Branch: A Bulletin of the Federal Courts* (January 1980), *12*:5.

46. Burger, Warren E. (September 24, 1971). State of the Judiciary—1970. Reprinted in *Congressional Record*, 92nd Cong., 1st sess., 117, p. 15012.

47. Interview with Alice L. O'Donnell, (July 7, 1972). coordinator for interjudicial affairs, Washington, D.C.

48. Burger, Warren (July 5, 1971). Remarks before the American Bar Association. Reprinted in *Congressional Record*, 92nd Cong., 1st sess., 117, p. 15013.

49. Rosenberg, Maurice (January 1980). Interview in *The Third Branch: A Bulletin of the Federal Courts 12*:4.

50. Flagg, Ronald S. (December 1976). *Stone* v. *Powell* and the New Federalism: A Challenge of Congress. *Harvard Journal on Legislation 14*:170-171.

51. A more moderate view is held by McGowan, Carl (Spring 1978). Federal jurisdiction: legislative and judicial change. *Case Western Reserve Law Review 28*:554-555.

52. *The Third Branch: A Bulletin of the Federal Courts* (June 1980). *12*:3.

53. Meador, Daniel J. (Spring 1978). Are we heading for a merger of federal and state courts? *The Judges' Journal 17*:9,46,50.

5

Intergovernmental Authority Costs

Jerome J. Hanus   The American University, Washington, D.C.

Federal, state, and local governments in the 1980s are entering an especially dynamic period of institutional change. Three factors, in particular, are largely responsible for this development. One is the stringent fiscal position in which the nation and many of the states have found themselves; the second is a popular perception of the federal government as inept and intrusive; and the third is the election of Ronald Reagan as president at the beginning of the decade.

These factors have already had an important impact on one dimension of federal-state relations which has become increasingly controversial since the 1960s: the use of federal regulations to subordinate state and local government to national directives. This chapter will describe the existing network of regulations, the political elements which sustain it, its impact on governmental authority, and recommendations for reforming the network.

THE NETWORK OF INTERGOVERNMENTAL REGULATIONS*

As it was in so many social areas, the 1960s was a watershed in the history of intergovernmental relations (IGR) [1]. This can be shown most dramatically by recounting a few statistics. In the early 1960s there existed 160 grant programs costing $7 billion. Compare this with the $90 billion in 1980 which

*The term "network" is used here instead of the more conventional term "system" to emphasize the characteristics of program entanglements and incremental growth.

wended its way through 500 grant programs to 37,000 of the 38,000 state and local governments. If this latter figure merely constituted federal subsidization of specific activities which Congress had designated to be in the public interest, criticism would have been oriented toward the efficiency and effectiveness of the programs. But there arose another dimension to these programs which, though unremarked for some time, distinguished the late 1970s from earlier decades.

While promotion of activities thought to be in the national interest continued to mark intergovernmental aids, less emphasis was placed on attracting the cooperation of subnational governments and more on requiring them to perform designated tasks [2, 3]. Researchers have found this to be the case, for example, in programs involving environmental protection; elementary, secondary, and higher education [4]; strip mining; weatherization; and occupational health and safety [5]. These federal mandates are orders or conditions-of-aid, the violation of which can, at the discretion of the federal government, deprive the recipient of a benefit. Such mandates now pervade the intergovernmental network. Researchers at the University of California at Riverside found, for example, that local governments participating in federal and state grant-in-aid programs could be subject to as many as 1200 federal mandates (most of which were imposed after 1965) [6].

These mandates can impose substantial fiscal costs on the subnational governments. Mueller and Fix of the Urban Institute found in their study of six grant-in-aid programs in seven jurisdictions that the "incremental cost of mandates, on the average, equalled the total revenue sharing funds received by the seven jurisdictions. . . ." [7]. Nationwide, they estimated the costs of administering the six programs to be over $7 billion [8]. New York City officials have estimated that the city is regulated by 47 federal and state mandates which will impose, between 1980 and 1984, costs of "11 billion in capital expenditures, $6.25 billion in expense-budget dollars, and $1.66 billion in lost revenue" [9]. One may argue whether this is too much money or too little, but there is no escaping the fact that mandates include substantial fiscal costs.

TYPES OF MANDATES

While several researchers have offered fairly elaborate typologies of mandates [10, 11], for our purposes the elemental categorization in Figure 1 will suffice. A direct order is immediately imposed on the subnational government commanding it to do or not to do some specific act, such as meeting clear water standards and orders issued by a federal court. A condition-of-aid is a provision in a grant which must be performed if a grant application is to be accepted or if the grant is to continue.

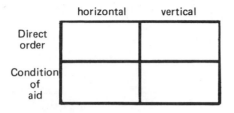

Figure 1 Types of mandates.

Vertical mandates are those "directed at one function, department, or program" [12]. They are usually procedural requirements which specify how an activity must be performed. An example is the requirement in the Weatherization Assistance for Low-Income Persons program that employes must be CETA workers. A horizontal or crosscutting mandate is not related directly to the purpose of the grant or program but is attached to it often from the moment of application by the applicant.

As the Lovell study showed, most of the federal mandates are horizontal, and each can apply to a large number of programs. The study also showed that most federal mandates are derived from administrative regulations and that most of them are conditions-of-aid rather than direct orders [12]. A recent study by OMB counted 60 policy and administrative requirements which automatically attached to financial assistance, or grants-in-aid, to the states. These include non-discrimination laws, environmental protection statutes, the National Historical Preservation Act, the Davis-Bacon Act, public participation requirements, and various OMB (Office of Management and Budget) circulars designed to standardize information dissemination and auditing procedures [13]. A direct relationship does not exist, however, between any one category of mandates and the benefits or costs of the mandates within the category. But there is a consensus among writers on the subject that it is the horizontal mandate which is most onerous to the recipient and the type toward which complaints are most frequently directed.

Both types of mandate have additional submandates which detail the way in which the primary ones are to be applied. Submandates specify such matters as definitions of employment discrimination, forms of compliance and enforcement, utilization of sanctions, conduct of investigations, training, data- and record-keeping procedures, types of publications, work-sharing projects, memoranda of understanding, job standards and qualifications, and descriptions of staff and resource needs [14].* Consequently, there is often little

---

*According to the Federal Paperwork Commission, federal reporting requirements ran to $5 billion in 1977.

discretion in the administration of programs exercised by subnational governments.

Overlapping federal jurisdictions compound the problem. For example, 32 federal agencies administer the 82 federal equal employment opportunity mandates and 17 agencies administer the Civil Rights Act of 1964. Each agency requires a slightly different reporting form from state and local governments and, because these are horizontal mandates, the specific requirements attach to every federal grant program. Not surprisingly, the result is often confusion and delay [14].

Two federal programs illustrate the variety of constraints imposed on state and local government. The Rehabilitation Act of 1973 is the source of several horizontal requirements imposed on recipients of federal financial assistance (including state governments). The act prohibited discrimination against, or denial of benefits to, otherwise qualified handicapped individuals by any federally funded program inclusive of all grants-in-aid. Each federal agency was required to develop and promulgate regulations to carry out the purposes of the act. In the meantime, Executive Order 11914 gave responsibility to the Department of Health, Education, and Welfare (HEW) to coordinate the regulations promulgated by the various agencies. The regulations applied not only to direct but also to indirect recipients of federal financial assistance and to any of their *successors* to such assistance. State-administered programs affected included those involving library, vocational education, community service, old-age assistance, and community health.

Among the regulations to which states and other recipients must adhere are

Prohibition of the use of criteria which have the purpose or effect of defeating or substantially impairing accomplishment of the objectives of the recipient's program with respect to handicapped persons, or which perpetuate the discrimination of another recipient of federal funds if both recipients are subject to common administrative control or are agencies of the same state

Denial of the right of a recipient, in determining the site of a facility, to make selections that have the effect of excluding handicapped persons

Assurance of compliance with regulations obligating the recipient for the entire period of assistance to ensure that the subsidized facilities are used for the purpose for which federal assistance was extended

Authorization of the director to order a recipient to take remedial action with respect to handicapped persons who are no longer in a program or who would have been in a program if the discrimination had not occurred

Requirement of a recipient employing more than 15 persons to designate at least one person to coordinate efforts to comply with the act's prohibition of discrimination

Requirement that a recipient design programs to make them readily accessible to handicapped persons by such methods as redesign of equipment and reassignment of services to accessible buildings

Dozens of other regulations have been issued by HEW affecting recipients, but no special funds have been made available to assist recipients in
complying with their grants (although monies from the grants themselves may
be used for that purpose). One may reasonably assume that grant applications
have been inflated to meet these increased costs, thus effectively reducing the
money available nationally for the primary purpose of the specific program.

The Weatherization Assistance for Low-Income Persons program provides another equally vivid illustration of the complex mesh of requirements in
grant-in-aid programs. The program was designed to operate via grants to state
and local government agencies which have had their applications accepted by
the regional administrator of the Department of Energy (DOE). To be eligible,
a state had to submit a plan within 90 days of the publication of rules by DOE.
The state plan must have been preceded by one or more public hearings on the
proposed state plan. The plan itself must encompass some 25 factors, such as
the type of weatherization work to be done, mechanisms for providing sources
of labor, estimates of the number of eligible dwelling units in which the elderly
and the handicapped reside and the extent to which they have priority, the
amount of nonfederal resources committed to the program, and an assurance
that funds will be allocated to a Community Action Agency (CAA) unless the
governor of the state determines that the CAA is ineffective. However, a local
applicant may request that the state plan's allocation not be implemented and
that DOE's regional representative determine the allocation and priority of
funds instead. In addition, each grantee must ensure that federal funds will not
supplant state or local ones; that the grantee must be "sensitive" to the problems of low-income people; and that the grantee have an advisory council
which includes representatives of the elderly, handicapped, and low-income
Native Americans. Altogether, program regulations consume 11 double-column
pages in the Code of Federal Regulations. Many of the regulations refer to
other federal documents containing additional requirements.

SOURCES OF FEDERAL MANDATES

The sources of such federal mandates as described above are Congress, administrative agencies, and the federal courts. But, like most lawmaking in a pluralist
democracy, interest group activity plays an important role in initiating and
maintaining the intergovernmental network. Also, like other types of legislation, the dominant though not exclusive motive behind intergovernmental
programs is money. If one keeps in mind that each federal dollar requires the

commitment of three state or local dollars, then one begins to sense the pervasiveness of the federal presence and the opportunity for the exercise of federal influence. Although the funds are allocated by either outright grant or by formula, the politics involved are similar [15, 16]. Washington, D.C. is inundated with public pressure groups representing regions of the country (e.g., the Southern Growth Policies Board and the Northeast-Midwest Coalition), the cities (e.g., the National League of Cities and the National Conference of Mayors), the counties (e.g., the National Association of Counties), and the states (e.g., the National Governors' Association, the National Conference of State Legislatures; and individual state offices in the Capitol), all trying to obtain grants for their constituencies or attempting to introduce factors into the grant formulas which will benefit themselves. Like most interest groups, they work through their congressmen and senators, relevant subcommittees, and influential executive offices (including the White House) to ensure the continuation of existing programs and to press for their expansion.

Two rationales are put forth by the states to justify their grantsmanship activities. The first is that a program is needed but the subnational jurisdiction cannot afford to meet the need through its own financial resources. The second is that if subnational jurisdictions do not participate in the programs, they will lose the money which has been taken from their jurisdiction in the form of federal taxes. Taken together, these arguments constitute a strong motivation for state and local governments to participate in the federal programs.

The subnational jurisdictions are also buttressed by the power of private interest groups (e.g., construction companies, labor unions, teachers, tenants, and welfare recipients) that travel to Washington to lend their support to favored programs. There they engage in the typical forms of pressure group activity described above, with one exception. Many of these groups had lost their fights for benefits at the local and state levels and now seek to attain at the federal level what they had lost earlier—a typical example of Schattschneider's "socialization of conflict" [17]. Some particularly influential interest groups, ideologically oriented, press for crosscutting requirements rather than for funds per se. Examples of these are groups representing racial, gender, and handicapped interests.

It comes as no surprise, then, to discover that statutes and regulations contain certain provisions which reflect these special interests and, often, require their participation in implementing the programs. However, unlike most federal and state legislation, there is little organized opposition to any specific grant as such. Because the money is raised at the federal level but spent in legally independent local jurisdictions, the direct legislative connection between taxes and specific expenditures is broken. Thus taxpayers in Las Vegas, for instance, may be only dimly aware that they are paying for a waste treatment plant in Reno, even less aware that the plant is costing more than market value because of the federal vertical and horizontal mandates imposed, and unaware that the state authorities had earlier determined, rightly or wrongly, that it was of low priority within the state. Those who wanted the plant were concentrated in their efforts while opposition was diffuse at the national level. We shall return to this type of behavior pattern later in the chapter.

AUTHORITY COSTS

So far the kinds of costs to which we have been referring are largely economic. These costs are described most frequently in the literature on intergovernmental grants, and they are the ones which lawmakers most commonly address [18].* Even when President Johnson launched his policy of Creative Federalism and President Nixon his New Federalism, the justifications were usually framed in terms of efficiency and economy. The 1970s are particularly interesting because the rhetoric of the time left one with the impression that the national government had decentralized its control over the grant network at the same time that it was vigorously acting to achieve a considerable array of national objectives. But what is in danger of being overlooked is the extent to which the federal government actually preempted subnational decision making through statutory and regulatory mechanisms [19].† This section of the chapter defines the shift of traditional legitimate decision-making power from one governmental entity to another as an "authority cost" to the former.

Because authority was allocated by the Constitution almost 200 years ago, the only legitimate ways for rearranging that distribution are through constitutional amendment and Supreme Court decisions. To do so by statute or regulation without a firm basis in the Constitution is an illegitimate procedure in a federalist democracy and over time may reduce the respect with which the citizenry hold government. This constitutionalist perspective was described by Professor Wechsler 20 years ago:

> Issues of federalism . . . may not be made to turn on the material interest that is affected, be it that of labor or of management, producers or consumers, or whatever other faction is at bar. The relevant principles involve abstractions about state and central

*For an analysis of inflation costs on state and local governments emerging from grants-in-aid programs, see Ref. 18.
†For a thorough discussion of partial and total preemption, see Ref. 19.

government; they must do service in delineation of the governmental structure, whatever claims to power or advantage win political acceptance for the time. [20]

The point he makes is that the Constitution assumes the existence of strong state governments; therefore, the incremental, almost absent-minded, erosion of their position significantly affects the quality of our representative democracy. Less consequential changes which occur involve fiscal resources and administrative integrity (which, interestingly, are not much different from regulatory costs in the private economic sector) [21]. Part of the argument here is that the question of fiscal costs is less central to intergovernmental relations than the political costs. Yet the opposite assumption dominates the literature on the subject. What is necessary now is to show how federal dominance over state governments can occur.

Federal regulatory preemption has been legitimated in three ways. First, as noted above, it may be based on direct constitutional authority. Examples include matters relating to interstate commerce and the taxing and spending powers, all three of which are specified in the Constitution. These powers have been used to regulate private and state governmental activities. Although *National League of Cities* v. *Usery* (1976) emphasized that certain core functions of the state had a constitutionally protected immunity from federal control: "It is one thing to recognize the authority of Congress to enact laws regulating individual business necessarily subject to the dual sovereignty of the government of the Nation and of the State in which they reside. It is quite another to uphold a similar exercise of congressional authority directed not to private citizens, but to the States as States" [22]. Thus, a crucial distinction was made between regulation of the private sector and the public.

Second, regulation of a state may occur as a procedural condition for receiving a federal grant. Such conditions have usually been justified on the ground that they ensure fiscal and administrative integrity. Investigators, however, have found that a substantial number of the conditions circumscribe state discretion while being only remotely related to the purpose of the grant itself [23]. Federal administrators have frequently inserted provisions to encourage states to participate in the programs and to detail the *ways* in which the program is to be administered.

Third, regulation appears as a result of crosscutting requirements which attach to grants-in-aid but, as with procedural conditions, have little to do with the purpose of the grant. These are justified on the ground that it is an efficient way for the federal government to attain national objectives when it lacks the legal authority to do so through direct legislation.

One of the consequences of these developments, as political scientists

Dubnick and Gitelson have shown [24], is the increasing nationalization of state government during the past 15 years. Prior to 1965, most regulation and, therefore, decision making took place at the state and local levels, and the impact of such regulations was not visible beyond their limited jurisdictions. Nor were there significant authority costs to the polity because such regulatory authority was consonant with the traditional understanding of the Constitution. As originally conceived, the national government was to do relatively little except in certain specified areas, and the states a great deal. At least formally, authority and responsibility coincided with constitutional expectations.

On the other hand, social and economic conditions have changed significantly. As is frequently pointed out, grant-in-aid requirements have had a long history, American society is now but a single entity, and the American people have willingly cooperated in the movement toward nationalization. The implication of these arguments is that costs involved in centralization are trivial in comparison to the benefits. However, the two following examples suggest there may be more costs than expected if one goes beyond revenues and expenditures alone and that citizens, once they become acquainted with national regulatory activities, may not be as supportive of them as once assumed.

A recent study of a small town by the U.S. Regulatory Council found the following citizen perceptions of regulatory programs, both federal and state: (1) citizens saw little or no relation between regulation of their activities and the social objectives of the regulations, (2) lawyers and bureaucrats were seen as the chief beneficiaries of government regulation, (3) administrators were seen as being too rigid in their dealings at the local level, and (4) federal regulations were seen as saddling some communities with the burden of responding to problems arising elsewhere [25].

When things go wrong, citizens may neither be particular nor careful about whom they blame. Whether a counterproductive regulation was the responsibility of the federal or the state government, it is problematic as to which becomes the target of the citizen's anger or frustration. However, one might guess that whoever is seen as administering the regulation is most likely to be the target. If so, a state official merely carrying out federal requirements will probably have to bear the brunt of the complaints. This truly becomes a drain on the limited reservoir of authority which public officials possess in the United States.

The second example is drawn from the Occupational Safety and Health Act (OSHA), in which one can discern an extreme form of national preemption occurring. First, the act offers the state the opportunity to assume responsibility for the program. The federal government will pay 50% of the state costs for administering the program, *providing* the state meets or surpasses the federal standards developed by OSHA. The condition is important because the requirements are both detailed and burdensome.

The experience of South Carolina in bringing its laws and agencies into compliance illustrates its subordinate condition. It had to shift responsibility for administering health and safety coverage of agricultural employes from the State Department of Agriculture to its Department of Labor and most of its regulations for enforcement and review of contested cases had to be changed to bring them into conformity with OSHA requirements. Many of these changes required new state legislation before they could go into effect. Thus even the state's authority over its own organizational structure was in effect preempted by the federal government.

That the states have been of two minds about accepting the "carrot" of the 50% federal match is indicated by the fact that, after 10 years, only 21 states had decided to participate either partially or fully in the program. For those states participating, the authority costs have been significant (keeping in mind, especially, the controversial nature of the program): the preeminent symbol of representative government—the state legislature—has had to rewrite its laws to conform to federal administrative rules, governors have had to reorganize administrative departments to conform to OSHA regulations, and all state officials have quickly become aware that final decisions lie with a federal administrator. In addition, public anger at unpopular actions by any of the 21 states is often directed as much at the state itself as at OSHA. OSHA clearly contravenes the spirit of federalism, although unfortunately it is not the only one which does so.

What have been the consequences of programs similar to OSHA for state governments? First, as Levine and Posner have pointed out, "Federal grants entice state and local government participation and increase their expenditures for both economic and political reasons" [26]. Economically, a grant will lower the direct cost to the recipient (although less than would appear on the face of the grant). In a time of fiscal austerity this can be a significant, short-run attraction. Politically, by accepting the money, state decision makers are relieved of the charge that they are letting state tax money escape to the federal government and eventually to other states. An illustration of the authority costs incurred, however, is offered in a study of El Paso. The investigator noted that prior to its first revenue-sharing entitlement the city had received very little federal aid. With General Revenue Sharing, however, federal funds climbed from 2.4% of local revenues in 1972 to 19% in 1973 and 25% in 1976. The mayors of the city traditionally had not sought federal funds and were skeptical about them, but the "no strings attached" sales pitch for General Revenue Sharing persuaded them to accept the funds, and local politicians jumped at the chance to provide increased services to their voters.

Sixty-three percent of El Paso's General Funds budget eventually came from federal sources, and it became highly sensitive to federal policy changes. When countercyclical revenue sharing was not continued in fiscal year 1979, the city budget was thrown into disarray and the city's balanced budget requirement was violated. El Paso remained heavily dependent on federal funds, because raising local revenues to cover the costs of the vastly expanded local government activities was politically impossible.

Along with the fiscal costs came a reduction in the authority of El Paso city government. The Police Department had to change its flexible work assignment policy to satisfy equal employment opportunity mandates, and city agencies had to respond to federal auditors by changing their accounting and reporting procedures. Much local decision making subsequently shifted to Washington, D.C. or to a federal regional office. As the author of the study observed, "If the New Federalism has helped to make federal funding policy a factor in all taxing and spending decisions, as seems to be the case in El Paso, it can hardly be regarded as having promoted local independence from Washington" [27].

Second, interest groups find that the nationalization of decision making is appealing because they can attain benefits at the national level which are effectively blocked by taxpayers at the state or local levels. An example of this was the efforts in the 1970s by the National Education Association to avoid budget cuts at the school district level by lobbying for increased federal financial support of elementary and secondary education and by promoting federal regulation of education which would force the commitment of local resources if school districts wished to participate in the federal funding. Since opposition to federal regulation is usually diffused throughout the nation while proponents form a concentrated and intense group at the national level, much of the decision-making authority of both the state and the school district was indeed transferred to Washington, D.C. without an effective public debate taking place. Thus federal regulations imposed significant authority costs on the subnational governments.

Third, the political structure from which grant-in-aid programs emanate ensures dominance by spending-minded interest groups and by reelection-minded congressmen, which virtually guarantees the subservience of state and local elected officials who are locked out of the process. From a congressman's standpoint, grant-in-aid programs are pure gravy. They allow Congress to expand the scope of federal activities without incurring the wrath of taxpayers over a "bloated bureaucracy" because the increase in government employees takes place at the subnational level. Since most programs have a built-in matching requirement, it means that Congress can pass on significant costs to other governments. Revenue collection and expenditure functions are separated so that it appears that Congress is offering "free lunches" to the states. These two functions, which should be intrinsically linked and thus self-limiting, in fact result in two separate political structures in the Capitol. A ratchet effect occurs as the constituent groups—contractors, educators, welfare associations, the handicapped, the elderly, and so on—interact with like-minded subcommittees and federal bureaus to increase the funds and jurisdictions of their favored programs. Since the grant-in-aid programs are usually special purpose, the actors are virtually unchecked. One need not belabor the point that these groups do not regard the fiscal or constitutional integrity of government as a matter of overriding concern.

On the other side of the equation are the taxpayers. Generally, their interests are, if not protected, at least listened to by the congressional taxing and expenditure committees. However, their direct political influence is severely limited. Taxpayers are not concentrated in particular constituencies and there is no federal agency which provides them with consistent support (the Office of Management and Budget may do so on occasion, but it generally takes its cues from the current state of presidential politics). What should be the first line of institutional defense—the state and local governments—is effectively outflanked by shifting the battlefield to the national level. Only in those states in which there are provisions for voting on bonds or initiatives and referenda can the local public make its voice clearly heard.

Fourth, the way in which these programs are administered discourages state and local efforts from imposing expenditure controls. The flow of the administration of federal grants is from a designated federal agency, which may have only a half-dozen administrators involved in the program, through a "single state agency" (often a condition of the grant), to local public or private organizations operating at the field level. Once the grant is made, the state legislature or city council loses control over the funds (in most cases they will not even be able to control the decision to submit a grant application or to reject federal funds which are distributed by an entitlement formula), and the governor or mayor's office loses interest as their decisions affecting the program are now effectively precluded by the federal mandates. The effect of the administrative structure is to surrender control to the federal-state administrators and the clientele groups benefiting from the programs to the exclusion of local citizens opposed to it. This process has been euphemistically designated "picket-fence" federalism implying that, through bargaining, subnational administrators are able to protect the general interests of their respective jurisdictions.

Reality, however, falls short of this theory. Both federal and state administrators have a fundamental interest in continuing the programs, as do their respective interest groups. Both have strong incentives to diminish legislative and executive oversight, and neither have to worry about the increased taxes which supply the funds for the programs. But in this process, to ensure that federally established policies override state and local ones, without provoking extensive opposition from the latter, Congress weights the programs down with the crosscutting mandates referred to earlier. Because of they way in which the intergovernmental process is structured and the kinds of incentives built into it, it becomes very difficult for opponents or cost-conscious elected officials to intervene in the process. For example, 1980 Department of Education regulations governing bilingual education were estimated to add $591 million in costs, most of it falling on local school districts. As long as the districts wanted federal funds, they had to adhere to the bilingual regulations and thus accept the "bitter with the sweet."

We can now sum up the costs of grant-in-aid programs. (1) There is a strong tendency for them to inflate state and local program costs beyond what they would ordinarily be. (2) The programs increase the size of government bureaucracy at the state and local levels, although not at the federal. (3) Through program mandates, centralization at the national level is significantly increased. (4) The programs enhance the influence of special interest groups in initiating and maintaining programs which may have been opposed by a majority of citizens at the local level. (5) State and local policy making is distorted by being required to continue services or projects even though the problem originally justifying the grant may have been alleviated. (6) Substantial confusion and frustration by the electorate over whom to hold responsible for alleged waste or controversial actions which it encounters at the local levels. (7) Loss of respect for all government institutions, especially state governments, as citizens become aware that their votes in state elections may have only a marginal effect on the issues raised during the course of campaigns for state offices [28, 29].*

Of all the costs described, the most debilitating for American government are those which constitute authority costs. That is, those policies that detract from the formal power of government institutions specified in the traditional allocation of functions under the Constitution. These costs arise because of the assumption of state functions by the national government on the ground that they have become national problems which can be met only at the national level. Students of government regulation should take a closer look at this justification. An example of the possible weakness in such arguments may be found in the 55 miles per hour requirement imposed as an energy conservation measure on states receiving federal highway funds. Those who have driven the open highways of eastern Montana or Kansas or New Mexico realize that a national speed limit is unrealistic and tends to make scofflaws of western citizens. While

*On the problems of confidence and accountability, see Refs. 28 and 29.

the energy problem is indeed a national one, the response to it will affect parts of the nation differentially, not uniformly; consequently, in this policy area, state responses would seem to be most appropriate. Education is another policy arena (and a very emotional one—another reason for leaving it at the local level) which appears to be of national concern but which has inherently local characteristics. Many grants, therefore, while appearing to be reflecting national concerns, are merely disguised supports for special interests.

CONCLUSION

The types of factors described in this article characterized intergovernmental relations in the 1970s, and the agenda of the state and federal governments in the 1980s will contain substantial efforts to resolve intergovernmental problems. The three factors listed at the beginning of this chapter suggest why the attempts to rework the intergovernmental network may succeed where earlier ones failed. Undoubtedly the most important of these is the continuation of fiscal stringency at both the federal and state levels. The Reagan administration has taken a public position in favor of reassessing the efficiency of the network, and a surprisingly large number of Democrats have expressed sympathy with the effort. Unlike President Nixon, who tried to accomplish a similar objective, Reagan paradoxically has been assisted by a high level of public cynicism toward government in general and by the fact that, in addition to his conservatism in fiscal affairs, he views public authority from an ideology of constitutionalism. This ideology has been reinforced by a strong distaste for federal regulations as a result of his experience as governor. Consequently, whether or not Reagan is succeeded by a Republican, the momentum generated in the early 1980s will continue to be toward greater sensitivity toward subnational governments in the intergovernmental network.

A certain anomaly, however, will be evident in the reform measures. The horizontal or crosscutting mandates are the ones most frequently criticized in the literature, yet they are the least susceptible to political reform. Because many of them, such as affirmative action and aid to the handicapped, symbolize an apparent national commitment to various groups, no amount of research disclosing their lack of cost-effectiveness will lead to their curtailment. Consequently, reform efforts will be concentrated on vertical regulations. And, because most direct orders are court mandated and cannot be overridden by other branches of government, reforms will be oriented toward conditions-of-aid.

The Reagan administration's early proposals for block grants provide evidence of the pragmatic thrust of their efforts. Some of their proposals for eliminating maintenance of effort requirements, reducing reporting requirements,

standardizing accounting procedures, and attaching fiscal notes to new mandates were offered by prior administrations but had no legislative success [30].*
The momentum in the 1980s will undoubtedly result in the enactment of
many of these [31].† No matter how many procedural reforms are made at
the federal level to reduce the mandate burdens, the fundamental conflict
about who has the final authority to determine social, political, economic, and
moral relationships within the states will continue to exacerbate tensions
between the citizenry and its government. Resolution will occur only when the
states are willing to sacrifice federal financial assistance in order to maintain
their independent authority over their own legal jurisdictions. This, in turn,
would mean having a consensus among the state citizenry that enhancement of
state authority is more important than federal money and its conditions. Without such a consensus, a healthier approach may be complete preemption of
state functions by the federal government. Responsibility and authority would
then coincide, and citizens would be less frustrated by not knowing what level
of government was responsible for what decisions. Meanwhile, authority costs
should be given equal weight with other factors when evaluating the grant-in-
aid network.

REFERENCES

1. The "grants explosion" has been described most recently in Hale, George
   E., and Marian Lief Palley (1981). *The Politics of Federal Grants*, Congressional Quarterly Press, Washington, D.C., pp. 11-14.
2. Walker, David B. (1981). *Toward a Functioning Federalism*. Winthrop
   Publishers, Cmabridge, Mass., pp. 100-129.
3. Hanus, Jerome J. (1981). Authority costs in intergovernmental relations.
   In *The Nationalization of State Government* (Jerome J. Hanus, ed.).
   D.C. Heath and Co., Lexington, Mass., pp. 1-34.
4. See the following studies by the U.S. Advisory Commission on Intergovernmental Relations. *Protecting the Environment: Politics, Pollution,
   and Federal Policy*, GPO, Washington, D.C., 1981; *Intergovernmentalizing
   the Classroom: Federal Involvement in Elementary and Secondary Education*, GPO, Washington, D.C. 1981; *The Evalution of a Problematic Partnership: The Feds and Higher Education*, GPO, Washington, D.C., 1981.
5. Hanus, Jerome J. (1981). Authority costs in intergovernmental relations.

*For a list of thoughtful recommendations for reform, see Ref. 30.
†Although Congress responded to President Reagan's proposals in 1981 by
consolidating 56 categorical grants into 6 block grants, it also added to the
grants a number of conditions and mandates.

In *The Nationalization of State Government* (Jerome J. Hanus, ed.). D. C. Heath and Co., pp. 1-34.

6. Lovell, Catherine H., et al. (1979). *Federal and State Mandating on Local Governments: An Exploration of Issues and Impacts.* University of California at Riverside, Graduate School of Administration.

7. Muller, Thomas, and Michael Fix (1980). The impact of selected federal actions on municipal outlays. In U.S. Congress, Joint Economic Committee, Special Study on Economic Change, vol. 5, Government Regulation: Achieving Social and Economic Balance, GPO, 96th Cong., 2d sess., p. 327.

8. Muller, Thomas, and Michael Fix (1980). The impact of selected federal actions on municipal outlays. In U.S. Congress, Joint Economic Committee, Special Study on Economic Change, vol. 5, Government Regulation: Achieving Social and Economic Balance, GPO, 96th Cong., 2d sess., p. 328.

9. Koch, Edward I. (Fall 1980). The mandate millstone. *The Public Interest, 61*:42.

10. Lovell, Catherine H., and Charles Tobin (May/June 1981). The mandate issue. *Public Administration Review, 41*:318-331.

11. Dubnick, Mel, and Alan Gitelson (1981). Nationalizing state policies. In *The Nationalization of State Government* (Jerome J. Hanus, ed.). D. C. Heath and Co., Lexington, Mass., pp. 39-74.

12. Lovell, Catherine, and Charles Tobin (May/June 1981). The mandate issue. *Public Administration Review* 41:319.

13. U.S. Office of Management and Budget (1980). *Managing Federal Assistance in the 1980s.* Office of Management and Budget, Washington, D.C., pp. 20-26.

14. Hale, George, and Marian Lief Palley (1981). *The Politics of Federal Grants.* Congressional Quarterly Press, Washington, D.C., pp. 100-102.

15. Collella, Cynthia Cates, and David R. Beam (1981). The political dynamics of intergovernmental policymaking. In *The Nationalization of State Government*, (Jerome J. Hanus, ed.). D.C. Heath, Lexington, Mass., pp. 131-161.

16. Hale, George E., and Marian Lief Palley (1981). *The Politics of Federal Grants.* Congressional Quarterly Press, Washington D.C., pp. 49-67.

17. Schattschneider, E. E. (1960). *The Semisovereign People: A Realist's View of Democracy in America.* Holt, Rinehart and Winston, New York.

18. Break, George F. (Summer 1980). Fiscal federalism in the 1980s. vol. 6, *Intergovernmental Perspective*, pp. 10-14.

19. Zimmerman, Joseph F. (1981). Frustrating national policy: partial federal preemption. In *The Nationalization of State Government*, (Jerome J. Hanus, ed.). D. C. Heath and Co., Lexington, Mass., pp. 75-104.

20. Wechsler, Herbert (1961). *Principles, Politics and Fundamental Law.* Harvard University Press, Cambridge, Mass., p. xiv.

21. Hanus, Jerome J. (1981). Authority costs in intergovernmental relations. In *The Nationalization of State Government* (Jerome J. Hanus, ed.). D. C. Heath and Co., Lexington, Mass., pp. 11-13.

22. *League of Cities* v. *Usery* (1976). 426 U.S. 833.
23. Lovell, Catherine H., et al. (1979). *Federal and State Mandating on Local Governments: An Exploration of Issues and Impacts.* University of California Press at Riverside, Graduate School of Administration.
24. Dubnick, Mel, and Alan Gitelson (1981). Nationalizing state policies. In *The Nationalization of State Government* (Jerome J. Hanus, ed.). D. C. Heath, Lexington, Mass.
25. U.S. Regulatory Council (1980). *Regulation: The View from Janesville, Wisconsin and a Regulator's Perspective*, U.S. Regulatory Council.
26. Levine, Charles, and Paul Posner (Spring 1981). The centralizing effects of austerity on the intergovernmental system. *Political Science Quarterly 96*:70.
27. Hudson, William E. (Summer 1980). The new federalism paradox. *Journal of Policy Studies*, p. 905.
28. Advisory Commission on Intergovernmental Relations (1981). *An Agenda for American Federalism: Restoring Confidence and Competence*, GPO, Washington, D.C., pp. 78-100.
29. Sundquist, James L. (1981). The crisis of competence in government. In *Setting National Priorities: Agenda for the 1980s* (Joseph A. Pechman, ed.). The Brookings Institution, Washington, D.C., pp. 542-552.
30. Advisory Commission on Intergovernmental Relations, (1981). *An Agenda for American Federalism: Restoring Confidence and Competence*, pp. 108-156.
31. Barfield, Claude E., Jr. (September/October 1981). Unsnarling the federal grant system. *Regulation*, pp. 37-42.

6

Attacking the Myth of Uncontrollable Expenditures

Robert F. Carmody The American University, Washington, D.C.

The federal government is committed to moving toward a balanced budget. Programs on which state and local governments have come to depend are among the primary targets for cuts, with up to 12% across-the-board cuts proposed. The combination of "uncontrollable" expenditures and increasing commitments for defense often seems to leave discretionary domestic programs last in line. Can the "uncontrollables" be controlled in a way which will leave resources available for federal support of state and local governments? From the federal perspective, can states be held responsible for large block grants? Is there any simple mechanism for holding states accountable without extensive red tape?

This chapter will look at some ways other than a traditional budgetary analysis in which the seemingly endless growth in federal expenditures might be curtailed. It cannot begin to cover and analyze each aspect of the Reagan administration attack on the federal budget, but it will identify some of its major strategies. What it will address is how, beyond the budget, some major areas of *expenditure* can be controlled. In the time between the writing and the publication of this chapter, many specific budget issues will arise and be resolved between the president and the Congress. In conclusion, this chapter will suggest the preliminary outline of one approach toward delegating the responsibility for some major federal programs to state and local government with a minimum of red tape.

The control of federal expenditures is seen as a budgetary exercise. The budget is only one result of political forces, resulting in authorizing legislation

with statutory entitlements, cost-of-living increases, wage determinations, re-
tirement provisions, crosscutting requirements on agencies and contractors, regulatory and reporting requirements and, other provisions with cost implications.
In addition the budget must take into account the maintenance cost of federal
debt, of the installations structure, and of many monolithic bureaucracies. Real
expenditures are increased by such factors as laxity in cash control, the failure
to collect obligations due the federal government, loose administration of eligibility standards, and the unnecessary payment of default claims on federally
guaranteed loans. Ironically, most of these factors are outside the normal scope
of responsibilities of the new Inspectors General who are charged with saving
the government money by eliminating "fraud, waste, and abuse." They are also
outside the scope of what is normally considered budgetary and fiscal control,
yet in order to control federal expenditures, these substantive issues must be
addressed.

THE MYTH OF UNCONTROLLABLE EXPENDITURES

For years, the myth has persisted that growth in federal expenditures was in-
evitable and that most of that growth was uncontrollable. Many items in the
budget were regarded as "fixed" and others as "legislatively mandated." That
perspective is from an executive viewpoint. From the congressional perspective,
"sacred cows" exist only as long as Congress continues to worship them [1].
The reconciliation process has provided congressional budget cutters with a
tool which does not require the extended process of repealing substantive legislation to eliminate statutory "entitlements."

   As Brandon pointed out [2], from the point of view of an executive budget, there is no choice but to implement existing laws; but to a congressional
budget maker existing laws can be subjected to reductions as well as increases.
He perceives uncontrollability as a "correct assessment of the political bias
against reducing an existing benefit and focusing attention on larger or smaller
amounts of increase [3].

   The reconciliation process is not the only avenue of assault on the irresist-
ible forces behind growth in federal expenditures. Such an assault requires an
examination of many of the traditions, bureaucratic practices, and legislative
mandates which make the federal government so unwieldy and expensive. Even
some of the "cures" which are being promoted have significant potential cost
implications and cannot be adopted without unique new controls.

THE REAGAN ADMINISTRATION APPROACH [4]

The Reagan Administration has emerged with an impressive array of attacks on
federal expenditures compared with the Carter administration [5]. First, the

personalities are significant. David Stockman's brilliant and dogged perseverance makes one wonder if Don Quixote has been rewritten with a David and Goliath ending. The selection of the most effective budget-cutting team in government, that of Caspar Weinberger and Frank Carlucci for defense, reflects the fact that cost control is viewed as critical in an environment of increasing resources.

DEFENSE EXPENDITURES

The most significant areas of discretion in terms of the magnitude and timing of expenditures will exist in the defense area. The Department of Defense (DOD) is also the one arena in which OMB has been unable to fulfill its traditional review role. While all other agencies are subjected to a subsequent review from OMB, because of the complexity of the defense budget, the OMB review tends to be concurrent with the DOD review. Both the expertise and the political power of the military and civilian leadership of DOD tend to overwhelm OMB examiners, even though they may be exceptionally competent. If fiscal restraint is to be exercised in DOD, it must come from within and from management which is in effective control of its own organizations. (The games by which the military neutralizes civilian managers are a part of a different story.) Another potential for cost savings with the administration is exploring is increasing pressure to get our alliance partners to assume a more significant share of common defense responsibilities. With the Special Analysis of the Budget predicting that defense expenditures will increase from $176.1 billion in fiscal year 81 to $257.5 billion in FY 83 and estimated at $258.0 billion in FY 84, the importance of cost control is apparent [6]. Here too is where the "camel in the tent" and long-term cost implications of major systems developments, such as the B-1 bomber and MX missile system, become especially significant [7]. Because of national priorities, if defense expenditures cannot be controlled, funds available for state and local governments will suffer. In addition, one of the most significant direct impacts on state and local governments of defense activities is the location of military installation and facilities, which will be addressed later.

One of the major uncontrollables in the defense area is Retired Military Personnel Pay, which amounted to $15.0 billion in fiscal year 1982. While the president could withdraw the opportunity to retire after 20 years, most military personnel perceive it as a right, and it is a sensitive issue when there is a military personnel crisis. There are also sensitive political issues surrounding the large number of retired military personnel receiving civil service salaries and the highest degree of job protection under veterans preference when the government is undergoing reductions in force. The issues of the military career system, military retirement, and "double dipping" will need to be addressed during this administration but they are in the category of sacred cows which have not yet been officially nominated for sacrifice at the altar of economy.

ENTITLEMENTS AND THE MAJOR UNCONTROLLABLE ITEMS

At the beginning of the second session of Congress in January, 1980, *Congressional Quarterly* pointed out that over 75% of the federal budget was committed to the "massive uncontrollable spending programs" called entitlements and to other forms of uncontrollable spending, and that the prospect of cutting them significantly was unlikely [8]. It quoted then Rep. David Stockman as saying that the situation threatened to turn Congress into "a green eye-shaded disbursement officer who totes up the bill, writes the check, and then trundles off to the chapel to mourn" [8]. Much of the remaining 25% was intended for national defense and federal employes' pay, which appeared to leave little real flexibility.

Entitlement programs result from authorizing legislation which identifies what recipients are eligible and provides a formula for determining how much is to be paid each class of recipients, whether institutions or individuals. The executive branch merely executes the laws and makes the payments called for. If either the appropriation is inadequate or the allocation made to a state or agency disbursing the funds is insufficient, Congress has generally provided a supplemental appropriation or additional funds have been allocated to the disbursing agency. The statutory language "shall" generally indicates that the recipients are "entitled" to the funds. Indeed, it was successful litigation initiated by recipients when the Nixon administration impounded funds in entitlement programs which enhanced their reputation as uncontrollable. An apparent entitlement may be limited by the availability of funds if the statute provides that the expenditures shall be made "only to such extent or such amounts as are provided in appropriations acts" [8].

The two largest uncontrollable items in the federal budget are Old Age and Survivors Insurance, the basic social security program, which approached the $155 billion level in fiscal year 82 (including over $18 billion for disability payments, and interest on the public debt, which cost $82 billion in fiscal year 82. The Reagan administration commitment to a basic "safety net" minimized the inevitable furor over any threat to Social Security as did its commitment to the long-term financial viability of the system (which many perceived as more threatening than limiting benefits). The administration succeeded in curtailing the minimum payment, higher education benefits, and other "non-safety" net features and generally tightening up eligibility, but it has had to defer fullscale reform.

The administration is planning attacks on other entitlement areas by streamlining current benefit formulas. The initial targets were savings of $2.6 billion in 1982, $10 billion in 1983, and $15 billion in 1984. The targets for these cuts included welfare (AFDC),which cost $7.3 billion in 1980; unemployment insurance ($15.8 billion); civil service retirement ($23 billion); food stamps ($6 billion); Medicaid ($14 billion); and other programs such as student aid and loan and school lunch programs. The attack on the child nutrition program ($3.2 billion) immediately met effective resistance from the school lunch lobby [9]. Actual fiscal year 82 expenditures and final 1983 budget figures for these programs are unknown at this writing.

The figures will change with each administration initiative and congressional response. The real issue is what strategies are beginning to emerge in the attack on the once-sacred entitlement programs. The first is a revision of the statutory eligibility standards to get a more restrictive definition of those who qualify. Second is the elimination of related benefit programs which have been "tacked on" to the basic system (e.g., Social Security minimum payment, education expenses, and extended unemployment benefits). The third is the tighter administration of eligibility standards. The fourth is in the recovery of overpayments when they are discovered. The tight regulation of benefit programs may run counter to some of the "deregulation" efforts, but restrictions in eligibility standards are not effective unless they are tightly administered. Personnel savings in some of these areas may actually be counterproductive if they eliminate employes who are saving the government money by reviewing and rejecting bad claims against the government, collecting debts owed the government, or collecting taxes.

LOAN GUARANTEE PROGRAMS

Loan guarantee programs have long constituted a significant amount of potential liability for the government. Current administration plans will curtail new guarantees and save some current funds. The big potential for short-term savings is in maintaining strict claims standards. In the last few years millions of dollars in claims in the Guaranteed Student Loan Program have been paid on an "expedited" basis subject to postaudits which may never occur. Millions of dollars in claims are paid every year with inadequate reviews because of staff limitations. In the past tight claims standards have been frustrated by the policy of "encouraging participation." With an administration objective of reducing volume, pending claims should receive the strictest review, and claims still subject to review should be screened. Similar concerns may apply to HUD (Housing and Urban Development), VA (Veterans Administration), and other loan guarantee programs. The economies that will result from staff cuts in these areas are miniscule compared with the potential cost to the government.

DEBTS OWED THE GOVERNMENT

The government's debt collection efforts, with the exception of the IRS (Internal Revenue Service), are ineffective. Collection staffs have suffered greatly from personnel cuts. The ultimate collection agency, the GAO (Government Accounting Office), does not pursue any small debts and very few under $1,000. Litigation is rare, and the books are cleared by writing off debts rather than pursuing them. The potential for exercise of the government's right of offset is rarely exploited. The dismal record of the government in recovering funds paid improperly by it or owed to it also strengthens the case for strong controls on eligibility of recipients and initial payments. Once the government pays out money improperly, it rarely gets it back.

FRAUD, WASTE, AND ABUSE AND THE INSPECTORS GENERAL

The federal government has launched an attack on fraud, waste, and abuse. Rep. L. H. Fountain, chairman of the Intergovernmental Relations and Human Resources Subcommittee of the House Committee on Government Operations sponsored the Inspectors General Act, [12] which created Inspectors General in most federal departments and agencies. These officers have audit and investigative responsibilities in each agency and have additional broad responsibility for curbing fraud, waste, and abuse. The Inspectors General have considerable statutory independence. They make semiannual reports directly to Congress, can refer cases directly to the Justice Department for prosecution, and can be removed only by the president, who must explain his action to the Congress.

On March 26, 1981, President Reagan created the President's Council on Integrity and Efficiency to focus and improve on the administration's efforts to deal with the problem of fraud and waste in the operation of federal programs [11]. The council is chaired by the deputy director of OMB and is composed of all of the statutory Inspectors General and other officials.

With such a broad mandate and strong support from the president, some have predicted that millions of dollars can be saved by the federal government. In fact, there have been attempts in Congress to make specific percentage cuts in all federal agency budgets to capture the savings anticipated from the Inspectors' General efforts. Certain factors will inhibit the realization of this dream. Criminal prosecutions punish violators, but do not recover funds. In fact, the institution of criminal proceedings generally delays the government's civil fraud and false claims cases until the criminal case is over. By then the money may be in Switzerland or the corporation involved bankrupt or "collapsed." One person involved in federal assistance cases has actually written a book on the art of collapsing corporations.

With the notable exception of the IRS, no federal agency is very good at simultaneously prosecuting violators and protecting the government's financial interests. This is not the fault of the Inspectors General but is rooted in the courts, the Federal Rules of Criminal Procedure [12], and the traditional practices of the Justice Department. New procedures for proceeding expeditiously with both types of action are needed. As long as some courts continue to give token sentences and fines in white collar cases, heavy civil fraud judgments and double damages for false claims may be more effective sanctions. Fraud must be prevented, not just punished. This means strong regulation and control systems. The zeal to prevent fraud and program abuse is counterbalanced by a strong antiregulatory sentiment.

THE ADMINISTRATIVE SUPPORT SYSTEM

The management consultants and experts who have advised the federal government over the last few decades have been consistent in one recommendation, "Consolidate like functions." While it sometimes meant programs, it always meant administrative support, such as personnel, finance, contracts, purchasing, and travel.

The consolidated support organizations which result do not provide support or service, they "allocate resources" as they see fit. Line organizations become supplicants for services they used to provide for themselves. When the support staffs worked for the head of the bureau being supported, the bureau head told them what he/she wanted and they did it. Now they have been transferred to the central organization. Their former organization has its support staff taken away, but it still needs them. The new central organization demands that the bureaus do all the work. The documents requesting service are almost enough to do the entire job, but each intermediate level reviews them again. Service is, at best, slow and unresponsive. In short, "the further any support organization is from the unit being supported, the less responsive it is."

The administrative support organizations become sources of power because they control the resources. The management core survives reorganizations and invariably skims some personnel allocations for itself from every new program or activity which is authorized.

The problem is compounded with the governmentwide support organizations. The General Services Administration is the support organization for the entire government. It took over the buildings which agencies had built with their own appropriations and now charges them rent for them. It is the "mandatory source" for supplies and its self-service stores unwittingly provide school supplies and Christmas presents for the families of government workers. It has succeeded in standardizing items for government purchases and providing supply schedules which permit agencies to conduct separate competitions to establish prices for things which they all use. On the whole, it is slow, unresponsive, expensive and (because of industrial funding) beyond effective fiscal control.

Similarly, all government printing goes through the Government Printing Office. Congress gets good service. For everyone else it is ponderous, expensive, and slow. Since it is part of the legislative branch, the printing office has even less reason to be responsive to agency needs or to exercise its monopoly in a responsible manner. No attack on federal expenditures would be complete without an examination of these ponderous administrative bureaucracies and the inefficient processes and procedures they have institutionalized.

THE PHYSICAL FACILITIES INFRASTRUCTURE OF THE FEDERAL GOVERNMENT

The physical facilities of the federal military and civilian establishments represent an empire which has not been subjected to a systematic review since the 1960s, when Secretary of Defense Robert McNamara launched an attack on the extensive base structure of the military establishment. Posts, camps, and stations existed which had been developed to meet the "mobilization requirements" of the First and Second World Wars. Many installations existed from the Civil War, and even the Revolutionary War, times, typically around a classic parade ground. Air Force bases had been built around manned bombers being replaced by missiles, and first-generation missile complexes were becoming surplus. There was excess capacity in naval shipyards and army arsenals. Other installations had been concentrated in certain geographic areas because of congressional influence. This phenomenon is not limited to DOD; many other federal agencies and departments have installations whose existence represents some past exercise of political power, not current functional necessity.

There has not been a comprehensive "base closure" task force for years in either the military or civilian departments of government. The loss is not just administrative efficiency resulting from consolidation, and the reduction in operations and maintenance costs, but the lost tax base and economic development potential for local communities. Many installations take up extensive land areas and remove important taxable land from local tax rolls. Others make major contributions and cannot be closed without concern for the economic impact. Unique among federal agencies, the Defense Department has an Office of Economic Adjustment which coordinates efforts to provide assistance to communities affected by installations closures and contract terminations and helps to make actions which are economically sound more politically acceptable.

THE COST BURDENS ON FEDERAL CONTRACTORS AND GRANTEES

Federal contractors and grantees are required to expend a large percentage of their grant or contract funds on purposes which meet legislative and regulatory requirements but which do not contribute to their primary purposes. They need to develop environmental plans and equal opportunity programs, certify their payrolls, hire persons to perform regulatory functions, and expend funds for a number of purposes which do not contribute to the primary purpose of their contract or grant. Current governmental parlance refers to these as "cross-cutting requirements." Internal bureaucratic structural considerations of the agency awarding the grant or control are important. If the line organization has staff elements which "consider these factors," then the primary mission has precedence. If there are staff elements which must "sign off" before anything can be done, then the secondary considerations have veto power over the primary purpose. Numerous studies have emphasized the burden of federal contractors and the costs associated with compliance with requirements extraneous to what is necessary to do the job. In the OMB studies of Federal Assistance Programs under PL 95-224, the Federal Grant and Cooperative Agreement Act [13], there is an extensive analysis of federal regulatory requirements.

TURNING RESPONSIBILITY OVER TO THE STATES

After surveying some of the most wasteful aspects of federal government management, it may be even easier to support turning functions over to state governments as a panacea. Unfortunately, many state agencies are clones of the federal agency which has been feeding them because each program office has sought to create a counterpart. State agencies would, of course, get bigger, if they had the primary responsibility. Fifty state Departments of Human Resources or Education may not be any better than one large federal agency. Some state and local agencies are corrupt, some are incompetent, and some are both. The recent dismal history of the CETA program should introduce some reservations about giving large sums of money to state and local governments without much guidance or control. Some officials of the soon-to-be extinct Law Enforcement Assistance Administration kept lists of states in order of their degree of corruption. Most federal agencies with 100% federally funded assistance programs have found out that states have little incentive to maintain fiscal control when none of their money is involved. In addition, because federal funds, even revenue-sharing funds, are considered "soft" money, they tend to be allocated to the less essential projects for which state money has not been appropriated. The people administering these projects are more likely to be temporary or without state or local civil service status so that they can be terminated if and when the money stops. Whenever the federal government has provided or is committed to provide 100% of what a state spends for a certain purpose, there is no incentive for the state to provide for strict adminstration of the funds.

On the other hand, there are state governments like California and many others and cities like Dallas, Phoenix, and Los Angeles, which are far more professionally and efficiently managed than most federal agencies. With adequate incentives and a minimum of red tape they can and will manage federal funds effectively. Is there a simple measure of accountability which will cause state and local governments to administer federal funds responsibly? Yes. In major benefit programs such as welfare, unemployment compensation, and food stamps, audit could establish an "acceptable" level of ineligibles. Any amount found above the acceptable level in an annual sample audit would reduce the level of federal matching from 100% in the following year. Except for a definition of recipient eligibility, certain integrity provisions and a percentage limit on the amount of federal funds which could be used for administrative costs, federal regulations could be minimized. Minimum standards of procedural due process for recipients denied benefits would also need to be specified. Just as in the case of the audit exceptions under Title 1 of the Elementary and Secondary Education Act, the states would seek legislative relief from their accountability. Congress would need to make a clear commitment to some effective mechanism for control.

CONCLUSION

The reconciliation process has become one way in which Congress has been able to change the traditional pattern of conflict between authorizing and appropriations committees into one in which concerns over resource constraints dominate. A shift in public opinion has reinforced Congress' determination to get control of federal expenditures at the same time that the executive branch has launched its own assault. The result has been to change all the old rules and assumptions about uncontrollable expenditures.

However, a budgetary approach is only a beginning. Major substantive changes need to be made. Programs need to be transferred to the states, and the federal bureaucracies which administer them abolished. Escalator provisions which range from cost-of-living provisions to inflated comparability standards, such as those required by the Davis-Bacon Act, need to be examined. The formulas contained in entitlements need to be revised and then enforced. The physical facilities and the administrative support structures of the federal government need to be trimmed. The crosscutting requirements of federal grants and contracts need to be minimized. The contracting and systems acquisitions processes need to be controlled to prevent cost overruns. The claims and collections processes need to be made to work. A major assault on civil fraud and false claims needs to be initiated. The remaining sacred cows need to be examined to see if they still have a genuine base of public support. The ultimate result should be a smaller and more efficient federal government performing those functions which are necessarily federal and the resumption by the states of a more significant relative role in the system.

REFERENCES

1. Sacred Cows. *Congressional Quarterly* (CQ) *Weekly Report*, July 18, 1981 1248; Reconciliation. CQ, July 25, 1981, 1327; Reconciliation roundup. CQ, August 15, 1981, 1489.
2. Brandon, Richard (Nov. 11, 1980). The balanced federal budget for FY 1981. Paper presented to the Operations Research Society of America National Meeting, Colorado Springs.
3. Brandon, Id. at 5.
4. Major news magazines summarized budgetary developments at the beginning of FY 1982: Now the squeeze really starts and Who'll be hurt by new round of budget cuts. *U.S. News & World Report*, October 5, 1981, p. 22, Rough waters ahead. *Time*, October 5, 1981, p. 8, Running to stay in place. *Newsweek*, October 5, 1981, p. 24
5. *Budget of the U.S., FY 1982*, Vol. 1, Office of Management and Budget (OMB), Washington, Jan., 1981.
6. *Special Analysis of the Budget, FY 1982*, Office of Management and Budget (OMB), Washington, Jan., 1981.
7. Three books give excellent views of major systems acquisition: Fox, J. Ronald (1974). *Arming America*. Harvard Press, Boston; Gansler, Jacques (1976). *The Defense Industry*. MIT Press, Cambridge; Augustine, Norman R. (1978). *Augustine's Laws in Major Systems Development Programs*. Reprinted from *Defense Systems Management Review*. Aerospace Division, Martin-Marietta Corp.
8. Uncontrollable spending limits hill power of purse. Congressional Quarterly (CQ), Jan. 17, 1980, p. 117.
9. Reconciliation roundup. Congressional Quarterly (CQ), August 15, 1981, p. 1489.
10. *Report on the Implementation of the Inspector General's Act*, Committee on Government Operations, U.S. House of Representatives, July, 1981, GPO, Washington.
11. President's Council on Integrity & Efficiency, Memorandum of President Ronald Reagan, March 26, 1981.
12. *Rules of Criminal Procedure for the U.S. District Courts*, Committee on the Judiciary, U.S. House of Representatives, GPO, Washington, 1979.
13. Federal Grant and Cooperative Act, P.L. 95-224.

7

Some Thoughts on Hyperintergovernmentalization

Catherine H. Lovell   University of California, Riverside, California

It has become popular to decry the current operation of our intergovernmental system. Walker of the Advisory Commission on Intergovernmental Relations (ACIR), as the leading critic of the system, talks about "supermarbleization and hyperintergovernmentalization," "a system out of control," and about "the collapse of cooperative federalism and the substitution of a dangerously dysfunctional version in its place" [1]. Summarizing a 3-year, 11-volume study of the intergovernmental system, the Advisory Commission on Intergovernmental Relations in December, 1980, concluded that the "current labyrinth of countless intergovernmental relationships—with their multiple vertical, diagonal, curving, and haphazardly horizontal connections—is less functional than that of 1960" [2]. Collela of the commission put it even more strongly: "government has become a monster of excessively pervasive and inordinately complex proportions. . . . The proliferation of regulations and programs and the extreme intergovernmentalization of implementation have created a largely uncontrolled and unaccountable system—'Leviathan' ran amuck" [3].

Before we accept this diagnosis, I wonder if we should not examine it more thoroughly and ask further questions about its validity. Some thoughtful intergovernmental scholars disagree with these global diagnoses. Nathan, for example, does not believe that the federal aid system is fundamentally flawed "despite the din of organizations and experts who obviously do not agree" [4]. He refers to the ACIR and related diagnoses as the "Henny Penny"

school of federalism [4, 5]. In the nursery school story, Henny Penny was willing to accept Chicken Little's conclusion that the sky was falling.

Is the intergovernmental sky really falling? Although popular right now,
the belief that it is may be based on form not substance, on values not facts.
Every observer agrees that intergovernmental relations have become exceed-
ingly complex, and are getting more so, and that the federal role has, in ACIR's
terms, become bigger, broader, and deeper. Whether or not the increased complexity and the enlarged federal role are dysfunctional, however, are not necessarily questions of fact (although empirical studies of real events are necessary
as a basis for interpretation) but are questions of values—values about the
proper role of government, about the worth of particular programs, about organizational and political arrangements, and about deciding which forms are
"effective" and which are not.

THE CURRENT DIAGNOSIS

In a recent bibliographical essay on intergovernmental change Anton divided
the current concerns being expressed by analysts about contemporary American
intergovernmental relations into three categories. For some analysts, he said,

> rapid growth in public expenditures is a major problem, either be-
> cause such growth implies a reduction of personal freedom or be-
> cause it is said to be accompanied by undesirable shifts in power
> relationships between levels of government. For others, the pro-
> liferation of new public programs at all levels of government has
> created a governmental system so complex that meaningful ac-
> countability of officials to citizens has been destroyed, leading to
> increased citizen apathy and decreased public trust in government.
> For still others, program proliferation accompanied by increasingly
> dense and frequent governmental interaction has created an "over-
> load" problem, characterized by decreased governmental capacity
> to achieve stated objectives. [6]

Walker in his recent book elaborates these three themes. He characterizes
the national government's role since 1960 as regulator, reformer, and promoter
of social and environmental goals as "vastly more assertive," and as having "expanded even more massively than it did during and after the New Deal" [7].
He sees the states assuming a much more assertive stance in revenue raising, in
aid programs to local governments, in assumption of new and sometimes previously local functions, and in regulating local governments. These state actions,
when combined with those of the federal government, he says, "have given rise
to an overloaded system," in which the national government provides few direct

services but conditions the delivery of services by subnational governments through funding and attendant regulations "thus raising serious questions regarding efficiency, effectiveness, equity, and especially accountability" [7]. He defines our current intergovernmental system as convoluted and overburdened.

Walker talks in some detail about vastly accelerated federal promotional activities, about growing federal government activities, about the national government assuming more policy and fiscal responsibilities for an ever-expanding range of governmental services and activities, and about ever-expanding federal regulatory efforts. He talks of "expansionist policy making" and its separation from "actual policy execution," and about the "growing gap between national policy goals and those emerging from the political processes of state and local governments" [8]. He sees the separation of policy making and policy execution and the federal-local policy goal gap as the chief reasons for what he summarizes as "dysfunctional federalism" [8]. For Walker, "federalism, if it means anything, means a rough but real division of labor." What he terms the current confusion at all levels as to their respective functional roles and the congestion at the center and at the peripheries results in "increasing dysfunctionality" [9].

Walker finds the intergovernmental system *administratively ineffective*. It is a "labyrinth of geometrically expanding vertical, diagonal, and horizontal linkages," with "massive fragmentation of administrative responsibility among programs, agencies, and governmental levels." He finds it *fiscally inefficient,* with duplication of aid programs, too much specificity in some grant programs, and increasing opportunities for fungibility in others, increased bypassing of states by federal-local direct relations, skewing of local budget priorities, and overstimulation of local spending [9]. He also finds it *politically dysfunctional*, with a "critical cluster of static attitudes and practices in the area of national policy implementation," which stand in dangerous tension with "the dynamic expansion in national public agenda items, the interest-group-dominated enactment process, and a steady reliance on subnational instrumentalities for program implementation" [10]. In sum, he finds the current "nonsystem," as he characterizes it, as "feebly functioning, poorly programmed, badly managed, inadequately accountable, and expensive" [11]. For him, the system itself is in question. "Its traditional and much vaunted traits of functionality and flexibility are at stake" [12].

All observers would probably agree with Walker that the intergovernmental universe in the United States has been transformed in the last 2 decades. Some see the transformation as incremental, others as radical. As Kirlin puts it, once largely autonomous governments now find themselves enmeshed in an intergovernmental system in which virtually no public policy of any significance is the decision of a single jurisdiction; from revenue generation through personnel processes and organizational design to decisions concerning service delivery, *all* is intergovernmental [13].

All observers would not agree with Walker that the transformed system which we find today is basically dysfunctional, although most would agree that some reform is necessary as dysfunction is present in all living systems. Anton, for example, says, "the global pessimists who suggest that the sky is falling seem to us singularly unpersuasive" [14]. If there is a "problem" of intergovernmental change, he says, it is primarily intellectual. He thinks that we neither know enough about patterns of interaction to sustain judgments about what the changes really are, nor do we possess conceptual frameworks adequate for the task of organizing complex behavioral "data" into "knowledge." His assumption is, however, that the changes are neither radical nor basically dysfunctional.

Walker has given us an impassioned, erudite, and intellectual global analysis of what he feels are the dysfunctionalities of the current system, but his discussion is remarkably silent about for whom the system is dysfunctional, what output values have been injured by his observed dysfunctionalities, and what the empirical bases are for many of his conclusions. As we move to an examination of his prescriptions for improving the system, some of the values which lie behind his definition of the situation as problematic may become more clear.

PRESCRIPTIONS FOR IMPROVEMENT

Walker's overall prescription calls for "rebuilding the system, itself" [15]. His prescriptions for doing that can be related to the three areas in which he sees the greatest dysfunction. In the first area, *administration*, he suggests decongestion and disengagement, which would be accomplished (1) through grant consolidations and eliminations, (2) through a more rational distribution of power and responsibilities among jurisdictions by devolving responsibilities for some programs to states or local governments and by fully centralizing both funding and administration of certain functions (such as welfare and unemployment compensation), and (3) through reduction of "excessive" use of conditional grants and curbing the regulatory and mandating activities of both the federal government and the states.

Walker would reduce jurisdictional fragmentation and generally restructure local governments by "strengthening them politically, administratively, and programmatically within the federal system as a whole and within the fifty state-local servicing and funding systems" [16]. He gives us no exact methods by which these prescriptions can be carried out, but their enunciation illustrates what must be an underlying value against which much of his analysis has been conducted. He clearly values a tidier, less complex system, with far fewer jurisdictions (particularly special purpose ones) and fewer fiscal transfer programs and attendant regulations. He appears to reject the idea that the necessary activities which must be carried out by governments in order to provide any service may usefully be thought of as three separate, but, of course, interrelated functions. The first is program development—deciding about the nature and type of service desired; the second is financing—paying for the service; and the third is actually delivering the program or service. A good deal of recent public administrative theory, as well as practice, suggests that the three kinds of activity—program development, financing, and producing—do not need to be done by the same organizational entity [17].* Alternative structural arrangements are possible for each of the three functions. In the traditional governmental model, which Walker seems to prefer, it was assumed that in order to deliver a service to the public we need to set up a governmental structure whose duty it is to decide what to do, to raise the money, and to provide the services with its own departments. In fact, this is no longer the typical governmental model, nor is it necessarily the most desired model. Increasingly, governments are working with and operating through other governmental and nongovernmental institutions to perform one or another of the three functions which make up program delivery, and increasingly the entities which perform each of the three components of program delivery are different. Cooperating relationships with division of the functions are both horizontal (such as intergovernmental contracting) and vertical (as in grant relationships and various cooperative agreements.)

The traditional model often assumes, as does Walker, that piecemeal, multiple arrangements are a problem and that duplication and overlap are evils. Empirically, however, we know that the need for unique structural arrangements for some kinds of services and communities can create problems when the deciding functions, the financing functions, and the production functions must be housed in one jurisdiction or in one government level. Problems are also created when all or most arrangements must look alike. It might be that the "nonsystem" of unique and varied sets of arrangements criticized by Walker is only problematic because it runs counter to our traditional model of neat, multipurpose governments which provide an array of services through a formalized decision system, financed by a sound, tax-based revenue system, and produced by one governmental level or department. The neat, single level, multipurpose government model contrasts strongly with existing situations almost everywhere in the United States (and in many other countries). Indeed, it could

---

*Ostrom was the first to make this explicit distinction.

be argued that a complex nonsystem responds quite well to the needs of today's disparate interests, widely different communities, geographical areas, and economic, ethnic, and social groups. In the United States our system responds to citizen needs through the use of some 60,000 formal units of multipurpose and special district governments, along with the use of hundreds of thousands of quasi- and nongovernmental institutions formed to respond to unique needs in unique communities.*

Walker and others, of course, decry the complexity of such a nonplanned system, with its seeming redundancy, overlap, and lack of formal, hierarchical accountability. Other observers, for example, Ostrom and Kirlin, would praise the participative opportunities, the responsiveness, the fail-safe qualities, and the pragmatism of a complicated mix of partially overlapping service systems [13, 17].

Once one accepts the idea that there is a choice of structural arrangements at each stage in the delivery of any given service, one is "freed up" to examine pragmatically which structures are available and seem right to meet unique situations, and one is loath to make blanket prescriptions [18]. Complexity and variety in structural arrangements may serve many "latent functions"; in fact, a hodgepodge of different arrangements may be useful for many purposes not always obvious at first appraisal (particularly if that appraisal is made from Washington and cannot focus on any one situation.) Although complexity and variety when seen through a national scope may seem to cause duplication and overlap, these attributes may cause service delivery to be more effective at the local level than it would be if it was "neatly" organized. One school of thought in contemporary public administration theory argues quite convincingly that the probability of failure or unreliability (lack of responsiveness) in a system decreases exponentially as redundancy and overlap factors are increased [19, 20]. It argues that it is more irrational than rational to greet the appearance of complexity, duplication, overlap, and "messiness" by automatically moving to excise and redefine. In its opinion, a variety of institutions and administrative arrangements can provide the redundancies and the unique arrangements that allow the delicate processes of mutual adjustment and self-regulation to function responsively and creditably. Moves to define or assign functional areas by system level, to obtain unity of command, to reduce intergovernmental negotiation, to streamline, and to consolidate functions may be more disturbing than helpful and should be undertaken with great care. The key problem, of course, is to distinguish between inefficient, unreliable, debilitating redundancy, complexity, and differentiation in grant or organizational

*I have intentionally used the number 60,000. Anton points out that of the 81,000 units of government we usually refer to, there are less than 60,000 that are actually operational.

arrangements and those that are constructive and contribute to increased responsiveness and reliability.

An empirical response to Walker's concern about increasing governmental fragmentation provides evidence of continuing changes in governmental structure with a great deal of attention being paid to the issue each year state by state. Between 1942 and 1977, according to Anton, some 93,000 school districts were eliminated, and some 2000 townships disappeared [21]. At the same time, nearly 18,000 new special districts and 2642 new municipalities were created. On the average, over 3300 government changes of some kind were made each year in the 3 decades. Anton contends that the continuous changes in structure represent a record of dynamic reformism not a system "run amuck" down the road to fragmentation. Anton also raises cautions about Walker's concern about proliferation of grant programs and supermarbleization by pointing out that although the number of federal programs and federal grants has indeed increased, the basic structure of the federal grant system is nevertheless not nearly as overwhelming as the numbers suggest [22]. Although there are about 600 programs providing financial assistance to state and local governments or to individuals through the states, only 100 of them provide fully 95% of the total grant funds available. As he puts it, it is "hardly an impossible number to comprehend" [22].

Walker's concern about overregulation or overmandating of administrative procedures is shared by many, including this author [23]. The problem, of course, is to examine in detail which conditions of aid (both crosscutting and those confined to individual programs) can and should be abolished or reformed.

Walker's second area of grave concern is the fiscal area. For him, the public sector is too expensive and, above all, badly managed and inadequately accountable. His overarching prescription appears to be that the federal government should spend less money, or at least spend money less foolishly. He urges elimination of doubtful, if not debilitating, programs, and he would restore the capacity to deny funds to the fanciful, the foolish, and the freeloaders. He would like the fiscal restraint debate to lead to a sobering sorting out of what "managerially, fiscally, and ethically is within the reasonable and realistic reach of the national government" [12]. He would reduce reliance on transfer payments and devolve tax sources. At no point does Walker indicate what particular programs represent his candidates for elimination. Individual value systems would of course be the basis for determining what should be cut.

Anton suggests that there is utility in "moving beyond the rhetoric of excessive federal spending to examine the beneficiaries of that spending" [24]. He quotes an analysis by Schultze which demonstrates that nearly 90% of the growth in the ratio of domestic federal expenditures to GNP (gross national product) between 1955 and 1977 was accounted for by just three types of federal activity. More than half the growth was traceable to social security, disability insurance, and unemployment compensation payments to individuals; 14% of the growth was for programs of assistance to low-income families; and nearly 20% was for new social service and social investment programs [25]. In Schultze's words it is the social investment grants-in-aid that have been "lightening rods for most of the criticism of domestic spending." Unfortunately, it is hard to know what the "global pessimists" about the system, like Walker, would classify as "fanciful and foolish" programs and who, they term, are the "freeloaders" in these three program areas.

We do know that the public sector in the United States (federal, state, and local governments combined) consumes a smaller portion of the GNP than does the public sector in most other advanced industrial countries. We know, also, that we have had a fiscal capacity-service need mismatch which has led to the need for transfers of money from the federal government to local governments. Revenues have continued to centralize in the federal government and needs for services have continued to grow at the state and local level. Tax limits being placed on local governments have exacerbated the mismatch.

Walker advocates "revenue turnbacks" to states and local governments which could help ameliorate the mismatch. As a recent Advisory Commission publication points out, there are four broad major alternatives for doing this: revenue sharing on a formula basis, tax sharing on an origin basis, conditional relinquishment of a federal tax, and unconditional relinquishment of a federal tax [26]. Although there are positive possibilities in some of these methods, there are, as the ACIR study points out, some rather serious barriers standing in the way of their operationalization. The most telling is the fiscal alignment problem, due to the fact that some states and localities are much more dependent on federal aid than others and are much below the norm in their ability to raise revenues from their own sources and finance increased responsibilities. The second barrier to tax turnbacks is the fiscal stress that the federal government now finds itself under since it has made political decisions to cut its own taxes and increase military spending. The federal government may be unwilling to share any tax sources. The third barrier is political; a turnback package cannot be put together without congressional and state and local agreement on what responsibilities should be turned back and what grants should be eliminated. There would also be political fights over the terms, the strings that must be attached to any turnback, either programmatic or fiscal, such as maintenance of effort and so forth. At any rate these proposals will be likely to get some serious consideration under the present administration.

Walker's third set of concerns is the *political dysfunctionality* of the present system, which he characterizes as "political overload." He finds political parties to be weak; functional, social, and moralistic interest-group activity to hold powerful sway in designing grant programs and conditions-of-aid; generalists in the system to be thwarted; and cooptive politics based on a contemporary adaption of traditional logrolling to be the dominant order. His prescription is more humility and less pretence at running things on the federal part, less federal regulation, and a greater recognition of what is now expected fiscally and managerially of the states. In general, he urges a fiscal, programmatic, and political strategy of "decongestion and of some disengagement within the intergovernmental system" [27]. He feels that the time is ripe for political reform and that some basic fiscal and program priorities can be established at the national level with the "sloughing off of the petty, the parochial, and the patently nonnational concerns that clutter the congressional agenda" [28]. He urges the checking of the aggressively assertive actions of special interest groups. These are broad-brush prescriptions; no details are given for how they are to be put into effect.

CONCLUSION

In conclusion, I would like to urge us to question carefully the pessimists who decry in global terms the present state of our intergovernmental system. Certainly there has been expansion in the complexity, scope, and size of intergovernmental activity. Certainly there has been (1) a dramatic increase in federal grants-in-aid programs and a major increase in direct federal-to-local programs, (2) increased dependency by local governments (particularly cities) on the federal government, (3) an increase in conditions-of-aid as aid has increased, and (4) an increase in more direct regulatory interventions. At the same time there has been increasingly active participation by state and local officials in political processes and in negotiations about the programs that affect them. In short, the intergovernmental system has become more complex and active. Its characterization in pejorative terms as supermarbleized, that is, hyperintergovernmentalized, overloaded, and dysfunctional, seems to be doing a disservice to some of the more subtle reform needs and to be leading us right into the den of Foxy-Loxy (who in the end gobbled up Chicken Little, Henny Penny, and the rest of the barnyard friends).

It seems that in Kirlin's terms, it is crucial to maintain an intergovernmental system capable of implementing a variety of policy strategies and capable of nurturing its diversity and flexibility [29]. That means working toward reforms in our system which empower the lowest levels of government, yet developing systems of articulated variety as needed to pursue broader policy objectives [29]. We are not going to turn back the clock to simpler, less overloaded systems. We must learn by careful thought, theoretical development, and empirical study how to understand, live with, and improve the complex intergovernmental system (both administrative and political) that will remain with us. To shout that the sky is falling leads to simplistic solutions like massive budget cuts and massive doses of deregulation in which worthwhile guidelines are thrown out with the bad. Not only will a lot of people get hurt in the process, but political and administrative systems will not necessarily be improved.

REFERENCES

1. Walker, David B. (1981). *Toward a Functioning Federalism*. Winthrop Publishers, mass., pp. 226, 228.
2. Colella, Cynthia Cates (Fall 1979). The creation, care, and feeding of Leviathan: who and what makes government grow. *Intergovernmental Perspective*, Advisory Commission on Intergovernmental Relations, pp. 6-11.
3. Advisory Commission on Intergovernmental Relations (June, 1981). *The Federal Role in the Federal System*, Washington, D.C.
4. Nathan, Richard P. (May 18, 1981). Reforming The Federal Grant-in-Aid System for States and Localities. Speech presented to the National Tax Association.
5. Anton, Thomas J. (January, 1980). Intergovernmental Change in the United States: Myth and Reality, ms., University of Michigan.
6. Anton, Thomas J. (January, 1980). Intergovernmental Change in the United States: Myth and Reality, ms., University of Michigan, p. 3.
7. Walker, David B. (1981). *Toward a Functioning Federalism*. Winthrop Publishers, Mass., p. 192.
8. Walker, David B. (1981). *Toward a Functioning Federalism*, Winthrop Publishers, Mass., p. 220.
9. Walker, David B. (1981). *Toward a Functioning Federalism*, Winthrop Publishers, Mass., p. 221.
10. Walker, David B. (1981). *Toward a Functioning Federalism*, Winthrop Publishers, Mass., p. 242.
11. Walker, David B. (1981). *Toward a Functioning Federalism*, Winthrop Publishers, Mass., p. 245.
12. Walker, David B. (1981). *Toward a Functioning Federalism*, Winthrop Publishers, Mass., p. 246.
13. Kirlin, John J. (Sept., 1978). Structuring the Intergovernmental System. An Appraisal of Conceptual Models and Public Policies, ms. Presented at the 1978 annual meeting of the American Political Science Association, New York.
14. Anton, Thomas J. (January, 1981). Intergovernmental Change in the United States: Myth and Reality, ms., University of Michigan, p. 5.
15. Walker, David B. (1981). *Toward a Functioning Federalism*, Winthrop Publishers, Mass., p. 246.

16. Walker, David B. (1981). *Toward a Functioning Federalism*, Winthrop Publishers, Mass., p. 261.
17. Ostrom, Vincent (1971). In *The Political Theory of the Compound Republic*, Public Choice, Blacksburg, Va.
18. Lovell, Catherine (February, 1981). Evaluating Alternative Financial Transfer Forms. State of Alaska, Department of Community and Regional Affairs.
19. Landau, Martin (July/August, 1969). Redundancy, rationality, and the problem of duplication and overlap. *Public Administration Review*.
20. Ostrom, Vincent (1973). *The Intellectual Crisis in Public Administration*. University of Alabama Press.
21. Anton, Thomas J. (January 1981). Intergovernmental Change in the United States: Myth and Reality, ms., University of Michigan, p. 53.
22. Anton, Thomas J. (January 1981). Intergovernmental Change in the United States: Myth and Reality, ms., University of Michigan, p. 58.
23. Lovell Catherine, and Charles Tobin (May/June, 1981). The mandate issue. Public Administration Review.
24. Anton, Thomas J. (January 1981). Intergovernmental Change in the United States: Myth and Reality, ms., University of Michigan, p. 39.
25. Schultze, Charles L. (1976). Federal spending, past, present and future. In *Setting National Priorities*, (Henry Owen and Charles L. Schultze, eds.). Washington, D.C., The Brookings Institution.
26. Davis, Albert J. (Spring, 1981). Stage Two: Revenue Turnback. *Intergovernmental Perspective*, Advisory Commission on Intergovernmental Relations, vol. 7, no. 2.
27. Walker, David B. (1981). *Toward a Functioning Federalism*. Winthrop Publishers, Mass., p. 258.
28. Walker, David B. (1981). *Toward a Functioning Federalism*. Winthrop Publishers, Mass., p. 259.
29. Kirlin, John J. (Sept. 1978). Structuring the Intergovernmental System. An appraisal of Conceptual Models and Public Policies, ms. Presented at the 1978 annual meeting of the American Political Science Association, New York.

Index

ANNALS OF PUBLIC ADMINISTRATION

Editorial Boards and Affiliations